INTERNATIONAL DEVELOPMENT IN FOCUS

Managing For Learning
Measuring and Strengthening Education Management in Latin America and the Caribbean

MELISSA ADELMAN AND RENATA LEMOS

© 2021 International Bank for Reconstruction and Development / The World Bank
1818 H Street NW, Washington, DC 20433
Telephone: 202-473-1000; Internet: www.worldbank.org

Some rights reserved
1 2 3 4 24 23 22 21

Books in this series are published to communicate the results of World Bank research, analysis, and operational experience with the least possible delay. The extent of language editing varies from book to book.

This work is a product of the staff of The World Bank with external contributions. The findings, interpretations, and conclusions expressed in this work do not necessarily reflect the views of The World Bank, its Board of Executive Directors, or the governments they represent. The World Bank does not guarantee the accuracy of the data included in this work. The boundaries, colors, denominations, and other information shown on any map in this work do not imply any judgment on the part of The World Bank concerning the legal status of any territory or the endorsement or acceptance of such boundaries.

   Nothing herein shall constitute or be considered to be a limitation upon or waiver of the privileges and immunities of The World Bank, all of which are specifically reserved.

Rights and Permissions

This work is available under the Creative Commons Attribution 3.0 IGO license (CC BY 3.0 IGO) http://creativecommons.org/licenses/by/3.0/igo. Under the Creative Commons Attribution license, you are free to copy, distribute, transmit, and adapt this work, including for commercial purposes, under the following conditions:

Attribution—Please cite the work as follows: Adelman, Melissa, and Renata Lemos. 2020. *Managing for Learning: Measuring and Strengthening Education Management in Latin America and the Caribbean.* Washington, DC: World Bank doi:10.1596/978-1-4648-1463-1. License: Creative Commons Attribution CC BY 3.0 IGO

Translations—If you create a translation of this work, please add the following disclaimer along with the attribution: *This translation was not created by The World Bank and should not be considered an official World Bank translation.* The World Bank shall not be liable for any content or error in this translation.

Adaptations—If you create an adaptation of this work, please add the following disclaimer along with the attribution: *This is an adaptation of an original work by The World Bank. Views and opinions expressed in the adaptation are the sole responsibility of the author or authors of the adaptation and are not endorsed by The World Bank.*

Third-party content—The World Bank does not necessarily own each component of the content contained within the work. The World Bank therefore does not warrant that the use of any third-party-owned individual component or part contained in the work will not infringe on the rights of those third parties. The risk of claims resulting from such infringement rests solely with you. If you wish to re-use a component of the work, it is your responsibility to determine whether permission is needed for that re-use and to obtain permission from the copyright owner. Examples of components can include, but are not limited to, tables, figures, or images.

All queries on rights and licenses should be addressed to World Bank Publications, The World Bank Group, 1818 H Street NW, Washington, DC 20433, USA; e-mail: pubrights@worldbank.org.

ISBN: 978-1-4648-1463-1
DOI: 10.1596/978-1-4648-1463-1

Cover photo: © Mark Colton. Used with the permission of Mark Colton. Further permission required for reuse.
Cover design: Debra Naylor / Naylor Design Inc.

Contents

Acknowledgments vii
About the Authors ix
Abbreviations xi

Executive Summary 1

CHAPTER 1 Why Study Management in LAC's Education Systems? 5
Notes 13
References 14

CHAPTER 2 Managers, Structures, and Practices 17
Who the managers are in LAC's public schools 18
Organizational structures to manage LAC's schools and education systems 24
The supply and quality of education management practices in LAC 29
Notes 39
References 40

CHAPTER 3 How Management Matters for Education Outcomes 43
Day-to-day school management 44
Managing shocks in schools 48
Managers and management practices in the middle layers 53
System-level management and service delivery 54
Notes 58
References 59

CHAPTER 4 How to Improve Education Management in LAC 65
Strengthening selection processes for school directors 65
Provide training, support, and incentives 70
Aligning layers of the system 76
Notes 78
References 79

CHAPTER 5 Taking Stock and Looking Ahead 83
How to measure management as a catalyst for improvement 83
How management matters for education outcomes 84
How to improve management: Selecting, supporting, and aligning 85

An agenda for future research 87
References 88

Appendix 89

Figures

1.1 Higher quantity of schooling completed on average across Latin American and Caribbean countries than other countries at similar levels of development 6
1.2 Lower quality of education on average across Latin American and Caribbean countries than other countries at similar levels of development 7
1.3 High education spending in several Latin American and Caribbean countries when compared to income group averages 8
1.4 Substantial learning losses expected due to COVID-19 related school closures in Latin American and Caribbean countries 9
1.5 Substantial variation in school efficiency within and across Latin American and the Caribbean, suggesting room for improvement at current spending levels 11
1.6 Better managed schools are more efficient, producing higher student learning for a given level of measured inputs in Latin America and the Caribbean 12
1.7 Snapshot of the growing data on management and evidence of its importance in the education sector across Latin America and the Caribbean 13
2.1 Coexistence of multiple selection methods for public school directors, including merit-based competition and appointment by authorities, within Latin American and Caribbean countries 19
2.2 Substantial variation in the education level of public school directors across Latin American and Caribbean countries 20
2.3 Public school directors skew male when compared to teachers across Latin American and Caribbean countries 21
2.4 Public school directors start at a young age and stay in the post for several years in many Latin American and Caribbean countries 22
2.5 Many public school directors are supported by school councils or management committees across Latin American and Caribbean countries 23
2.6 Public school directors have more decision-making autonomy over practices directly affecting students than over personnel practices in most Latin American and Caribbean countries 25
2.7 The majority of public school directors have indefinite contracts with their schools across Latin American and Caribbean countries 26
2.8 Government-supported management training programs in selected Latin American and Caribbean countries are a good start but have substantial room for improvement in their organization, content, and delivery 28
2.9 Public school directors self-report dividing their time between many different tasks and stakeholders in Brazil, Chile, and Mexico 31
2.10 Substantial differences in actual, perceived, and ideal time allocation for school directors and pedagogical directors in childhood education centers in Brazil 32
2.11 Quality of school management practices in public schools varies substantially across and within countries according to the World Management Survey index 34
2.12 High prevalence of weak practices, yet important variation in the adoption of disaster preparedness and mitigation practices across schools in Haiti after a major hurricane according to a new School Disaster Management Survey index 36
2.13 Substantial variation in the incoherence of task allocation across and within countries according to a new Education System Coherence Survey 38
3.1 Increasing evidence of a strong positive correlation between school management practices and education outcomes in public and private schools across multiple measures and countries 44
3.2 Lower quality people management practices in public schools than private schools on average across Latin America and the Caribbean 46

3.3 Both people and operations management play a role in improving learning through selection and incentive channels   47
3.4 Well managed and poorly managed schools in Haiti were equally likely to be surprised by the impacts of Hurricane Matthew   50
3.5 Better managed schools damaged by Hurricane Matthew in Haiti reopened faster and had teachers and students back sooner than poorly managed schools   51
3.6 Better managed schools damaged by Hurricane Matthew in Haiti adopt better disaster preparedness and mitigation practices afterwards, while undamaged schools do not   52
3.7 Substantial variation in the *de jure* allocation of tasks, and in all cases, the minority of tasks are allocated to school directors across Brazil, the Dominican Republic, Guatemala, and Peru   56
3.8 Understanding of the *de facto* allocation of tasks across 10 core education functions shows substantial incoherence within education systems in Brazil, the Dominican Republic, Guatemala, and Peru   57
3.9 Negative correlation between the percentage of fully incoherent tasks and student learning at the school level in Brazil, the Dominican Republic, and Peru   58
4.1 Small yet stable positive impact of switching from municipal appointments to civil service examinations for school directors in Chile   68
4.2 Introduction of sit-in examination to select school directors in Peru had a short-term yet persistent negative impact on student value added across multiple cohorts in rural schools, but not in urban schools   69
4.3 Management training program increases student learning more in schools with directors who are smarter, younger, and with a higher sense of responsibility and perseverance in Houston, Texas   71
4.4 Results-based schools management training program in São Paulo, Brazil, shows significant positive effects on math scores of low performing students, but not on reading scores   72
4.5 Providing school leaders with user-friendly and timely data on student learning raises subsequent test scores, but adding capacity building did not help in La Rioja, Argentina   73
4.6 Focused support program for directors to keep children in school helps reduce dropouts in Guatemala, particularly for larger schools and for boys   75
4.7 Management capacity building program focused on aligning local actors to improve student achievement has had positive results across Brazil   78

Tables

2.1 Management practices measured in World Management Survey (WMS)   32
2.2 Management practices measured in the School Disaster Management Survey (SDMS)   35
2.3 Core functions of an education system measured using the Education System Coherence Survey   37
A1 Management practices measured across survey instruments   89

Acknowledgments

This study is sponsored by the Chief Economist Office for Latin America and the Caribbean (LAC). The initial stages of the study were completed under the overall guidance of Jorge Familiar (former Regional Vice President for LAC), Carlos Végh (former Chief Economist for LAC), Daniel Lederman (former Lead Economist in the Chief Economist Office), and Reema Nayar (former Practice Manager, LAC Education). The study was completed and published under the overall guidance of Martin Rama (Chief Economist for LAC), Elena Ianchovichina (Lead Economist in the Chief Economist Office), Emanuela Di Gropello (Practice Manager, LAC Education), and Luis Benveniste (Regional Director for Human Development in LAC). The study benefited from peer review comments from Ciro Avitabile (Senior Economist, World Bank), Nick Bloom (Professor, Stanford University), David Evans (Senior Fellow, Center for Global Development), Justin Sandefur (Senior Fellow, Center for Global Development), Sunčica Vujić (Associate Professor, University of Antwerpen), and two anonymous reviewers from the Latin America Development Forum. The authors also thank the participants in a 2018 authors workshop for feedback that helped shaped the study, and Yanina Domenella, Maria Jose Vargas, and Vicente Garcia for their research assistance.

About the Authors

Melissa Adelman is a Senior Economist in the World Bank Education Global Practice where she has led analytical and operational activities in diverse contexts, including the Democratic Republic of Congo, the Dominican Republic, Haiti, and Guatemala. Adelman also serves as a Thematic Lead on the topic of management capacity and service delivery for the Global Practice, advising teams and counterparts on school and system management issues. Before joining the World Bank in 2012, Adelman was a management consultant at Bain & Company in the United States and India. She holds a PhD in economics from Harvard University.

Renata Lemos is a Senior Economist in the World Bank Education Global Practice where she has worked on operations and analytical activities in Brazil, Colombia, Costa Rica, Ecuador, Mexico, Peru, and Uruguay. Lemos is a member of the core research team of the World Management Survey and her recent work focuses on topics in managerial and organizational economics in the public sector. Before joining the World Bank in 2016, she was a Lecturer in the Economics Department at Stanford University and a Research Associate at the Centre for Economic Performance, London School of Economics, and at Harvard Business School. She holds a PhD in land economy (applied microeconomics) from the University of Cambridge.

Abbreviations

CI	confidence interval
D-WMS	Development World Management Survey
DRM	Disaster Risk Management (Survey)
EGRA	Early Grade Reading Assessment
ESCS	Education System Coherence Survey
GDP	gross domestic product
IRT	item response theory
ITBS	Iowa Test of Basic Skills
JdeF	Jovem de Futuro
LAC	Latin America and the Caribbean
NGO	nongovernmental organization
OECD	Organisation for Economic Co-operation and Development
PDCA	plan-do-check-act
PISA	Program for International Student Assessment
PPP	purchasing power parity
SDMS	School Disaster Management Survey
SERCE	Second Regional Comparative and Explanatory Study
SMC	school management committee
SMTSI	School Management Training Survey Instrument
STAAR	State of Texas Assessments of Academic Readiness
TALIS	Teaching and Learning International Survey
TERCE	Third Regional and Comparative Explanatory Study
WMS	World Management Survey

Executive Summary

How can countries make sustainable gains in student learning at scale? This is a pressing question for Latin America and the Caribbean (LAC)—and the developing world more broadly—as countries seek to build human capital to drive sustainable growth. School access has expanded significantly, enabling nearly all children in the region to attend primary school; however, many do not gain basic skills and drop out before completing secondary school, in part because of low-quality service delivery. The preponderance of evidence shows that learning, not schooling in itself, contributes to individual earnings, economic growth, and reduced inequality. For LAC in particular, low levels of human capital are a critical factor in explaining the region's relatively weak growth performance over the last several decades. The easily measurable inputs are well known, and the goal is relatively clear, but raising student achievement at scale remains a challenge. Why?

Part of the answer lies in management—the managers, structures, and practices that guide how inputs into the education system are translated into outputs, and ultimately outcomes. Although management (and related concepts, such as institutions, governance, or leadership) is often mentioned as an important factor in education policy discussions, relatively little quantitative research has been done to define and measure it. And even less has been done to analyze how and how much management matters for education quality. This study begins to fill these gaps with new conceptual and empirical contributions that can be synthesized in four key messages.

Student learning is unlikely to improve at scale without better management. Individual interventions can succeed in the short run, but virtually any initiative or program—from coaching classroom teachers to providing school meals—requires effective management by public education systems, in addition to adequate financing, to reach the majority of children in LAC. Correlational evidence from within and across countries in the region and globally, coupled with a growing number of impact evaluations, show that higher-skilled managers and the use of more effective management practices can improve teaching and learning. Evidence from across countries participating in the Program for International Student Assessment (PISA) supports this idea: moving from the bottom to the top quartile of school management quality is associated with approximately an additional three months of schooling for one year alone. Furthermore, because individual managers or management systems affect relatively large numbers of teachers and students, the marginal cost per student of effective interventions can be very low while the internal rate of return is very high.

Management quality can be measured and should be measured as a catalyst for improvement. Capturing management processes and practices is not straightforward. However, several new instruments can now be used to consistently measure the quality of both the management within schools, including directors' time use and focus (from maintaining day-to-day school activities to dealing with shocks), and the management of the education system above the school level. These tools can support policy making in several ways: (a) they can provide snapshots of how well schools or systems are run to inform policy at the macro level, (b) they can identify specific practices that can be strengthened in programs and intervention areas, (c) they can track the impacts of changes in policies or programs on the practices of managers in the system, and (d) they can be used to enlighten managers about their own performance, providing feedback and opportunities for improvement. Moreover, thanks in part to growing participation in international standardized assessments and new measurement instruments, the availability of data on managers themselves and the organizational structures around them is also increasing.

Management affects how well every level of an education system functions, from individual schools to central units, and how well they work together. At the school level, better management can strengthen the daily learning experience by motivating teachers and students to put forward their best effort and enabling them with the support and inputs they need. Better management can also mediate the diverse shocks that schools face, from budget cuts to natural disasters, like the earthquakes and hurricanes common in LAC, to public health emergencies, like the current COVID-19 pandemic. At the system level, better managed units, aligned around a coherent allocation of responsibilities and common objectives, can deliver better services, such as getting teachers to the schools that need them and ensuring that buildings are properly maintained and adequate for learning. New conceptual and empirical research explores these channels and starts to identify the role of management in driving differences across schools, sectors (public and private), and countries.

Several pathways to strengthening management are now open to LAC countries, with the potential for significant results. Broadly speaking, emerging evidence points to three main approaches for strengthening management in schools and systems: improving selection processes for managers; creating or improving management career frameworks with training, support, and incentives; and aligning system actors toward delivering quality services:

- **Improving manager selection processes.** In countries across LAC and the world, many school directors are politically appointed without binding, merit-based criteria, or they earn their position solely by being the longest-serving teacher. These processes are not likely to reliably select for the skills and motivation needed to effectively manage schools and improve student outcomes. High-performing education systems globally take a purposeful approach to the development and selection of managerial staff. New research on the experiences of several recent policy changes in manager selection methods in Brazil, Chile, and Peru show that moving away from political appointments can change who is selected to lead schools and their subsequent performance. However, consideration of the quality of the candidate

pool, local conditions, and broader political economy are critical to the ultimate impacts of these reforms on student outcomes.
- **Developing and implementing practical, coherent training and support.** Much remains to be learned about effective managerial career frameworks, but emerging evidence suggests that practical preservice, induction, and in-service training programs that focus on specific practices tied to improving student outcomes can have sizable impacts on managerial practices and ultimately student outcomes. In the United States, an intensive, two-year in-service training in instructional leadership, delivered to school directors who remained in the same school for both years, raised student test scores by 0.15–0.30 standard deviations. In Argentina, providing school leaders with easy-to-understand learning data for their students and guidance on how to use those data raised subsequent student test scores by about 0.3 standard deviations. In Guatemala, a short, practice-oriented training program for school leaders focused on dropout prevention and reduced student dropout by 4 percent. Yet many government-supported in-service training programs for school directors take a broad approach, covering a wide range of topics with limited emphasis on practice, suggesting a need for more research on their effectiveness.
- **Better defining and allocating roles at all levels of the education system, and addressing incoherence.** In many LAC countries, the quality of services provided by public schools depends as much on the bureaucrats who sit above the school level as it does on school directors themselves. New data from Brazil, the Dominican Republic, Guatemala, and Peru show that when bureaucrats do not share a common understanding of their roles and responsibilities, student learning is lower. In Brazil, an impact evaluation found that a program to build management capacity that aligns school directors and local education managers around specific student achievement targets increased student test scores by about 0.1 standard deviations and was highly cost-effective.

Progress is possible within existing political economy constraints, but deeper reforms require strong political commitment. Given the negative economic consequences of the COVID-19 pandemic and near-term uncertainties, LAC countries do not have scope for large increases in financing. Some reforms are largely technical and can be adapted for existing structures. For example, clarifying allocation of responsibilities and articulating common objectives at each level of the system, or building school directors' capacity to provide effective (but essentially nonbinding) feedback to teachers, can have positive, cost-effective impacts with relatively modest investments. Other reforms, such as reallocating roles and responsibilities within a ministry or changing mechanisms for selecting managers, are likely to disturb entrenched interests and require significant political will to enact. Yet other reforms, such as developing and implementing new comprehensive training programs, require a real commitment of financial and technical resources. For all of these approaches, widespread awareness of the student learning crisis, coupled with the rapidly growing body of knowledge on management's role in addressing it, can help spur action.

This study elaborates on each of these messages, synthesizing recent data and research and presenting the results of several new papers that contribute research findings to this report. Chapter 1 presents the report's motivation, describing the context of Latin America's low average learning outcomes and fiscal constraints and the challenges shared by many countries beyond

LAC—of making systemic improvements in student outcomes. Chapter 2 describes new data collection instruments and descriptive data from LAC on managers, organizational structures, and management practices. Chapter 3 sets out a conceptual framework for management in education and delves into the channels through which management can affect student outcomes. The chapter highlights a new theoretical framework and supporting evidence on several elements: day-to-day management of schools; empirical evidence from Haiti showing that better managed schools are more resilient to shocks; and empirical evidence on how well public education systems function, with new data from Brazil, the Dominican Republic, Guatemala, and Peru. Chapter 4, building on the findings from chapters 2 and 3, describes new research on how to improve management from across the region, presenting the impacts of (a) changes in policies for selecting school directors in Brazil, Chile, and Peru; (b) different types of training programs for school management in Argentina, Brazil, and Guatemala; and (c) a program to align system actors toward common goals in Brazil. Chapter 5 distills the key messages of the research presented and identifies several areas for future work.

1 Why Study Management in LAC's Education Systems?

Since the late 1990s, countries in Latin America and the Caribbean (LAC) have made rapid progress in increasing the educational attainment of their youth (figure 1.1), with the average 18-year-old now having about 11.5 years of schooling (Adelman and Székely 2016; Bassi, Busso, and Muñoz 2015; Székely and Karver 2021). Access to education has expanded quickly, particularly at secondary and tertiary levels, facilitated by both public and private investment. This expansion has played an important role in helping people exit poverty and has contributed to the rapid growth of the middle class (Ferreira and others 2013). However, the average quality of education across the region is low, with all participating LAC countries scoring in the bottom half globally on math, reading, and science skills in both the 2015 and 2018 Program for International Student Assessment (PISA) results. When educational attainment is adjusted for learning, young people obtain the equivalent of only 55 percent as many years of schooling in Guyana and Haiti and 75 percent as many in Chile relative to what they would have attained if learning were maximized (World Bank 2018). As a result, LAC countries generally lag countries at similar levels of GDP per capita in educational quality (figure 1.2).

The preponderance of evidence shows that it is learning—not attainment in and of itself—that contributes to individual earnings, economic growth, and reduced inequality (González-Velosa, Rosas, and Flores 2016; Hanushek and Woessmann 2015).[1] For LAC in particular, low levels of human capital are a critical factor in explaining the region's relatively weak growth performance over the last half century (Hanushek and Woessmann 2012a, 2012b). Yet education systems have largely been organized around expanding coverage, with relatively little emphasis on quality or outcomes (Pritchett 2015; World Bank 2018).

A pressing question, therefore, is how to increase the quality of educational services and improve education outcomes. The easily measurable inputs are well known, and the goal is relatively clear, but identifying reliable approaches to improving student outcomes at scale remains a challenge. A large body of research has focused on analyzing the impacts of specific inputs—such as materials, infrastructure, and teachers—and concluded that there is substantial heterogeneity across contexts, not only in what improves student outcomes and

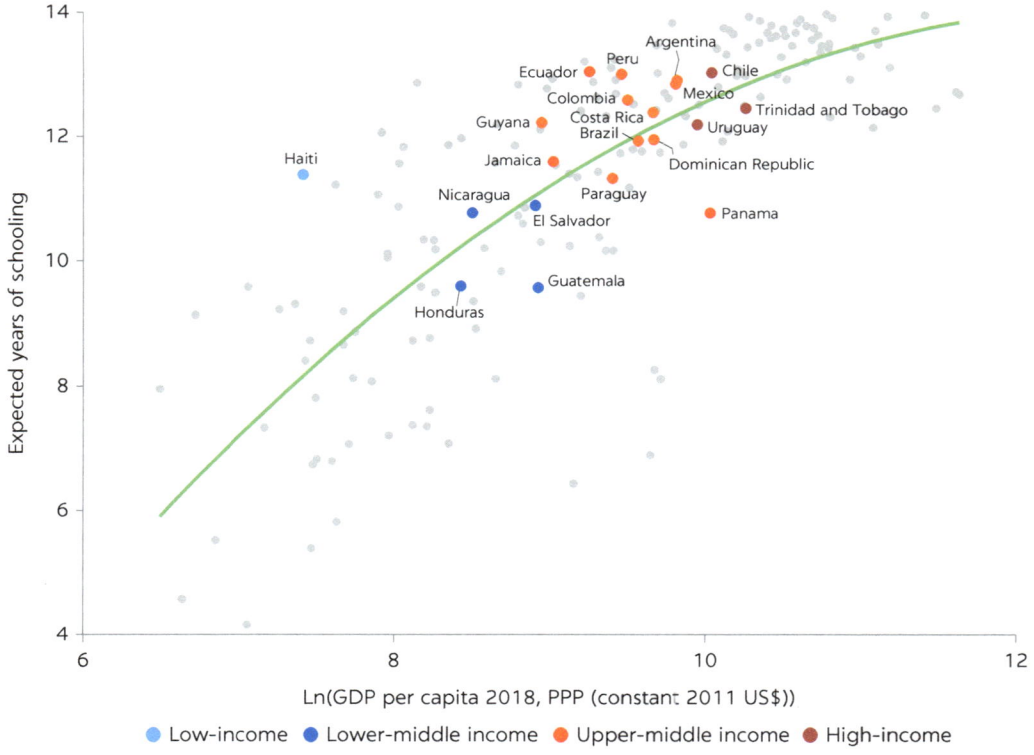

FIGURE 1.1

Higher quantity of schooling completed on average across Latin American and Caribbean countries than other countries at similar levels of development

Source: World Bank.
Note: The figure shows on the horizontal axis the log of country-level GDP per capita at purchasing power parity (PPP) in 2018, in constant 2011 US dollars (data from the World Bank International Comparison Program). The vertical axis shows the country-average expected years of schooling (data from the World Bank Human Capital Project). Countries in Latin America and the Caribbean are depicted by circles colored by income level; countries in other regions are depicted by smaller gray circles. The line presents the best fit, showing predicted expected years of schooling by GDP level.

what does not, but also in why (Glewwe and Muralidharan 2016). In a systematic review of reviews, Evans and Popova (2016) note that for some types of education interventions, the variance of effects is greater *within* types than across, making it even more difficult to draw general conclusions. Even additional financial resources provided directly to schools to spend on needs they identify themselves—which could be considered the most efficient approach—do not consistently affect learning outcomes (McEwan 2015; Ganimian and Murnane 2016). At the same time, interventions that work well when implemented by nongovernmental organizations (NGOs) or at a small scale have often failed to achieve any results when implemented by government (for an example of contract teachers, see Bold and others 2017).

Why is improving student outcomes at scale such a challenge? In this study, we argue that part of the answer lies in an understudied area in education: management.[2] Any initiative or program—from providing textbooks to coaching classroom teachers to offering school meals—requires both effective management

FIGURE 1.2

Lower quality of education on average across Latin American and Caribbean countries than other countries at similar levels of development

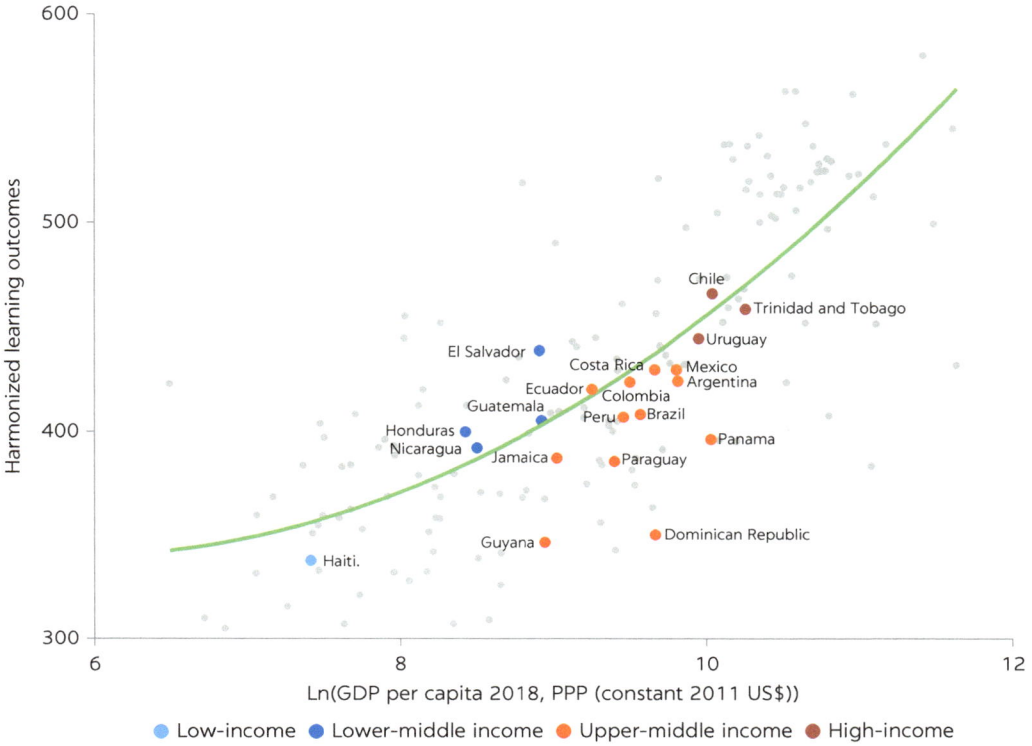

Source: World Bank.
Note: The figure shows on the horizontal axis the log of country-level GDP per capita at purchasing power parity (PPP) in 2018, in constant 2011 US dollars (data from the World Bank International Comparison Program). The vertical axis shows the country-average harmonized learning outcomes (data from the World Bank Human Capital Project). Countries in Latin America and the Caribbean are depicted by circles colored by income level; countries in other regions are depicted by smaller gray circles. The line presents the best fit, showing predicted harmonized learning outcomes by GDP level.

and adequate financing from the public education system to reach the majority of children.

Financing is certainly an issue, and of increasing concern due to the economic impacts of the COVID-19 pandemic. Although LAC countries spend on average 5 percent of GDP on education, in line with the Organisation for Economic Co-operation and Development (OECD) averages (figure 1.3), increasing demands for expanding coverage beyond basic education and providing higher quality services are stretching available resources. At the same time, declining commodity prices, slowing growth, and fiscal tightening have put pressure on public spending. LAC was already in a period of lackluster economic performance before the COVID-19 pandemic, and health and economic impacts are expected to push the region into a deep recession (de la Torre, Ize, and Pienknagura 2015; Végh and others 2018; World Bank 2013, 2020a). In this context of constrained financing, management—the practices that guide how inputs into the education system

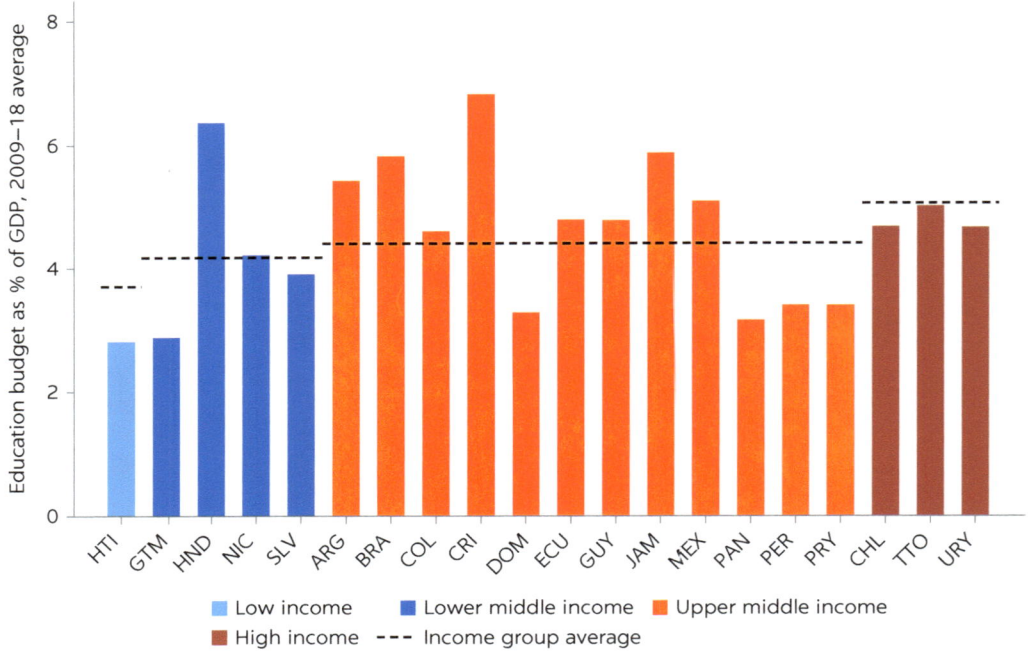

FIGURE 1.3

High education spending in several Latin American and Caribbean countries when compared to income group averages

Source: World Bank.
Note: This figure shows on the vertical axis average total government expenditure on education (as a percentage of GDP) for years 2009–18, when available. Data for the Dominican Republic comes from the World Bank's *Dominican Republic Public Expenditure Review Report, 2012–18;* data from Trinidad and Tobago comes from the Ministry of Finance's 2012–15 Estimates of Expenditure Reports; and data for all other countries are from the World Development Indicators database, United Nations Educational, Scientific and Cultural Organization Institute for Statistics. Dashed lines represent the average across all countries at each income level.

are efficiently translated into outputs and ultimately outcomes—is a particularly pertinent subject for LAC.

Moreover, the COVID-19 pandemic is creating new and acute challenges for school systems to manage. Countries across the LAC region and the world suspended in-person learning as an important public health measure, but it is a measure that threatens to undo recent progress and to exacerbate inequalities in education (World Bank 2020b). Nearly all public schools in the region were physically closed for at least five months following the initial outbreak of the pandemic, and many remain closed as of October 2020. While systems are working hard to expand remote learning resources, information to date suggests that many students, particularly the most vulnerable, have had limited participation in distance education. For example, a survey of selected Brazilian states suggests that although 74 percent of students were able to access remote learning resources, only 37 percent actually did (World Bank forthcoming). As a result, there will be a significant decrease in learning-adjusted years of schooling across countries (figure 1.4). Estimations show that students in LAC are expected to lose 0.5 to 2.1 learning-adjusted years of schooling, depending on the length of system closures. Returning to in-person schooling presents its own set of management challenges, as systems and schools work to implement health and

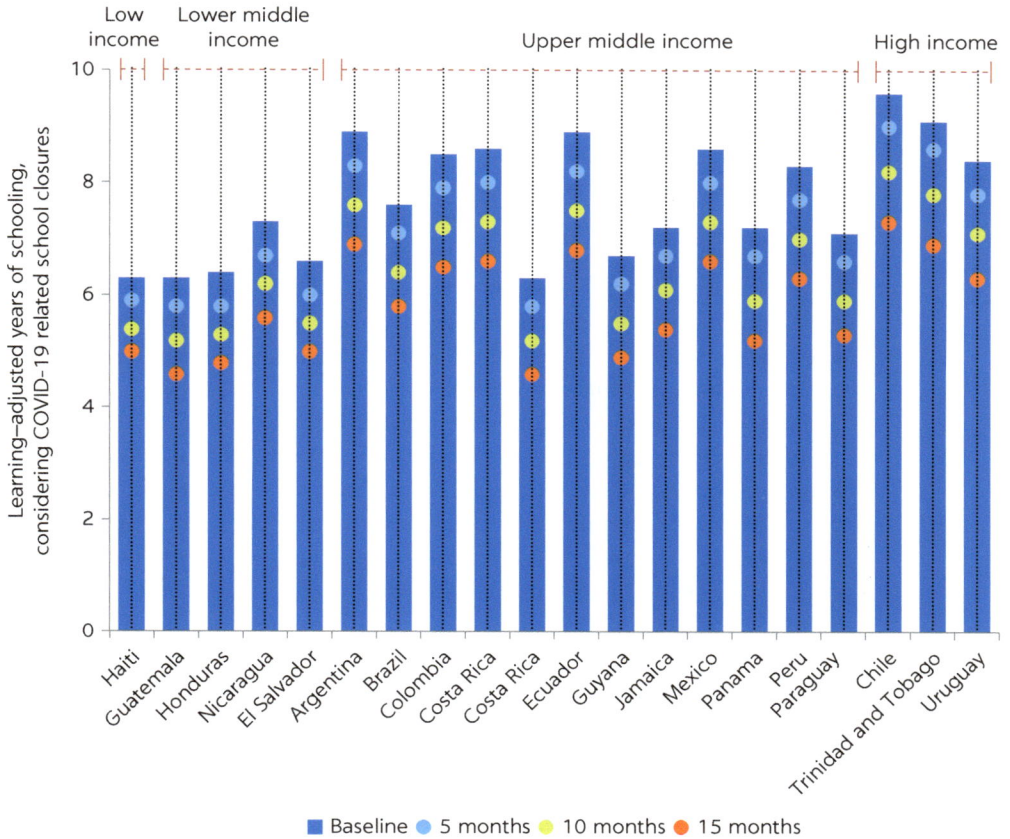

FIGURE 1.4

Substantial learning losses expected due to COVID-19 related school closures in Latin American and Caribbean countries

Source: World Bank LAC Education's COVID-19 Learning Losses Team using Azevedo and others "Country Tool for Simulating the Potential Impacts of COVID-19 School Closures on Schooling and Learning, version 5."
Note: This figure shows on the vertical axis estimations for learning-adjusted years of schooling across four scenarios. The bar shows the baseline using data from 2018. The dots show the optimistic, intermediate, and pessimistic scenarios corresponding to 5, 10 and 15 months of school closures, respectively. The parameters used match global simulations based on the country's income level group. Distance learning is assumed to be via the Internet. The school year is assumed to be 10 months in all countries. Across the region, average baseline of learning-adjusted years of schooling is 7.7 years, while the optimistic, intermediate, and pessimistic scenarios are 7.1, 6.5, and 5.8 years, respectively.

sanitation measures with limited resources; build trust among teachers, parents, and other stakeholders; and continuously adapt to the evolving pandemic (Harris and Jones 2020; WISE 2020).

Research on management in education is closely related to, and in certain respects an extension of, the broad literature on institutions and governance in education. The focus of this research has largely been on institutional forms, such as the level of school autonomy, the existence of standardized exam systems, and the extent of private sector competition.[3,4] Across countries, however, different institutional forms can produce similar student achievement results (and vice versa), and the effects of changing these forms depend heavily on the details of implementation (Pritchett 2015). Within LAC, a rich history of school-based management reforms in the late 1990s and early 2000s provides an example of how substantial variation in institutional forms may not produce very different student outcomes (Barrera-Osorio and others 2009; Bruns, Filmer, and Patrinos 2011; Di Gropello 2006).[5] Research in these areas is therefore moving toward more detailed assessment of the rules and resources within institutions, to the extent that data allow. For example, Hanushek, Link, and Woessmann (2013) find that increased school autonomy is positively correlated with changes in PISA test scores only in more developed countries, and negatively correlated in developing countries, possibly because of a lack of complementary accountability mechanisms.[6] In LAC, research on major policy changes to expand school choice, increase accountability, or increase support to schools shows a similarly nuanced picture. For example, the experience of Chile's voucher system has shown that increased competition alone was not sufficient to improve student performance, but reforms to the system that increased accountability along with financial and technical support to schools did have an impact (Murnane and others 2017).[7]

Outside of education, management has long been implicitly considered important in determining firm productivity across trade, industrial organization, macroeconomics, and labor economics, but only recently has it been explicitly modeled and measured. Bloom, Sadun, and Van Reenen (2017) lay out a theoretical framework supporting the view of management practices as a technology, in which specific practices raise total factor productivity, on average. This view is distinct from the view of management practices as a contingent feature of an organization, in which no practices are more productive than others but rather respond to the specific organizational environment (Gibbons and Roberts 2013). A small number of rigorous evaluations support this idea of management as a technology, showing that interventions to improve basic management practices can have large and at times lasting effects on productivity (Bloom and others 2013; Bloom and others 2020; Bruhn, Karlan, and Schoar 2018; Giorcelli 2019; Higuchi, Mhede, and Sonobe 2016).

A similar approach is now helping to advance management research in education, by defining and measuring school management practices and studying their relationship to student outcomes. This effort has been long in the making. For example,. Barrera-Osorio and others (2009) quote John Amos Comenius, a 17th-century Czech philosopher and early advocate of modern education, on the difficulties of developing and implementing school management methodologies. More recently, Bloom and others (2015) investigate whether practices in operations management, performance monitoring, target setting, and people management—which have been widely adopted in other sectors such as manufacturing, retail, and health care—are also used in schools across eight high- and middle-income countries. The authors find that across nearly all countries studied, such practices are less widely used in schools than in other organizations, such as hospitals and manufacturing firms. They also find that the quality of school management varies substantially, both across and within countries, and that quality itself is positively associated with school-level learning outcomes. For example, in the United States, specific school management practices, such as teachers giving frequent feedback and setting high expectations for student behavior, have been shown to distinguish successful charter schools from unsuccessful ones and from traditional public schools (Angrist, Pathak, and Walters 2013; Dobbie and Fryer 2013).

How much could be gained by improving education management across countries? To shed some light on this question, we start by conducting a cross-country efficiency analysis. We use data from PISA to estimate a regional efficiency frontier—essentially, the maximum amount of student learning a school in the region is observed producing given its measurable inputs—and to calculate the distance from that frontier for each school in the sample (efficiency scores), following Agasisti and Zoido (2018). Student learning is measured with the average school math and reading PISA scores, and inputs include the school teacher-to-student ratio; a standardized index of economic, social, and cultural status at the school level; and the computer-to-student ratio as a proxy for available technology at the school. Our results show substantial variation in efficiency within and across LAC countries (figure 1.5). On average, schools in LAC could produce one additional year of student learning, holding inputs constant, if they reached the regional efficiency frontier. We then correlate these efficiency scores with an index of school management

FIGURE 1.5
Substantial variation in school efficiency within and across Latin American and the Caribbean, suggesting room for improvement at current spending levels

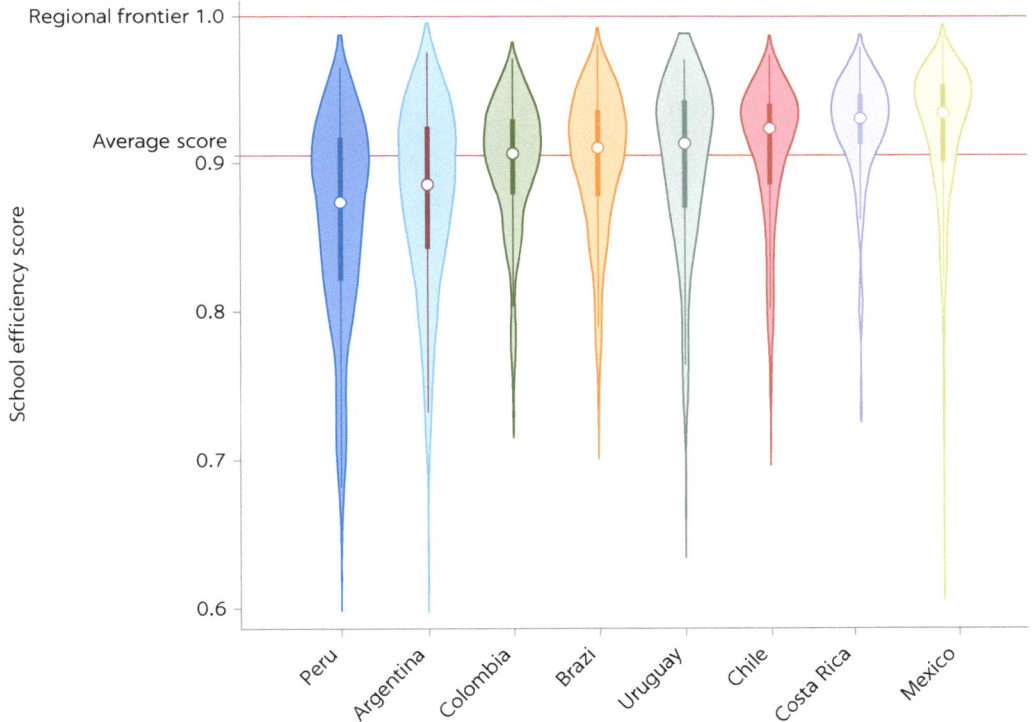

Source: World Bank.
Note: This figure shows the distribution of secondary (public and private) school efficiency scores within each country (a measure of the distance to the regional frontier) calculated using PISA 2015 data and following Agasisti and Zoido (2018). The white marker indicates the median value, the box indicates the interquartile range, and the spikes extend to the upper- and lower-adjacent values. An estimated kernel density is overlaid for each country. The regional frontier is set at 1, and the average school efficiency score is 0.92, indicated by the vertical red lines.

practices using the variables available in PISA, following Leaver, Lemos, and Scur (2019).[8] Schools' efficiency scores are strongly correlated with this index—a 1 standard deviation increase in management practices is correlated with a 0.1 standard deviation increase in efficiency scores—suggesting that investing in better management could potentially help schools increase student achievement across the region (figure 1.6).[9]

The remainder of the study synthesizes the growing research on management in education in the region, including new instruments to measure the quality of managers, structures, and practices, in chapter 2; evidence of how management matters for education service delivery and student outcomes, in chapter 3; and finally evidence of how to improve management, in chapter 4. This research comes from countries across the LAC region and provides a broad and promising base from which to further advance our understanding of how management matters in education (figure 1.7).

FIGURE 1.6

Better managed schools are more efficient, producing higher student learning for a given level of measured inputs in Latin America and the Caribbean

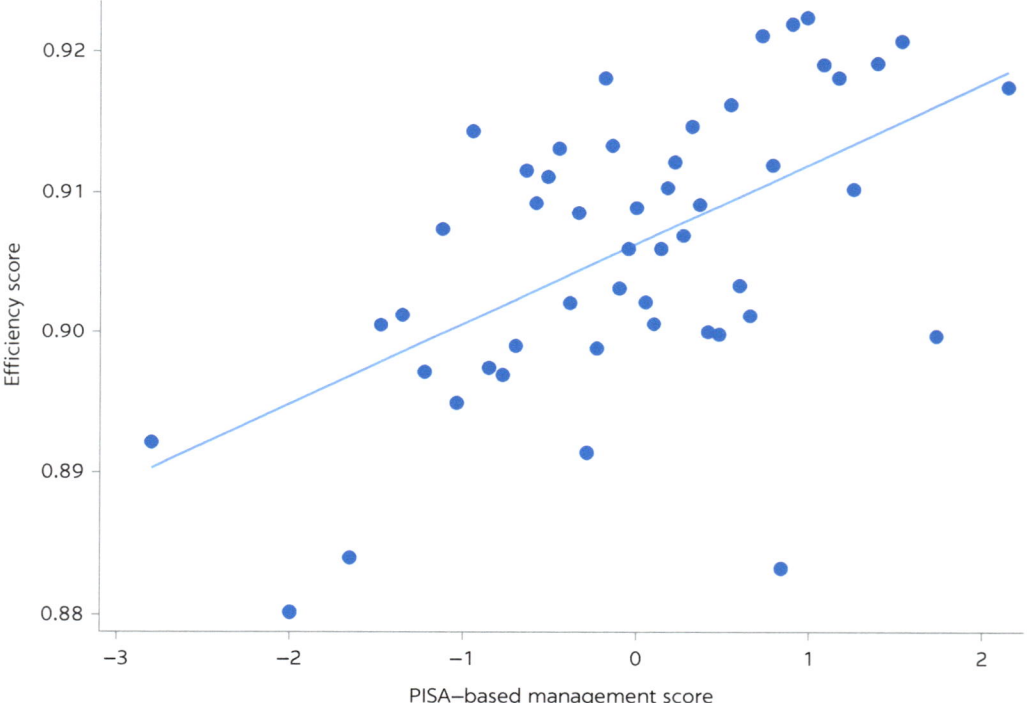

Source: World Bank.
Note: This figure shows on the horizontal axis the PISA-based management score (a measure of school management quality using the index in Leaver, Lemos, and Scur [2019]) and on the vertical axis the secondary (public and private) school efficiency score (a measure of the distance to the regional frontier calculated using PISA 2015 data and following Agasisti and Zoido [2018]). Data are plotted in 50 equal size bins of the PISA-based management score variable. The line presents the best fit.

FIGURE 1.7
Snapshot of the growing data on management and evidence of its importance in the education sector across Latin America and the Caribbean

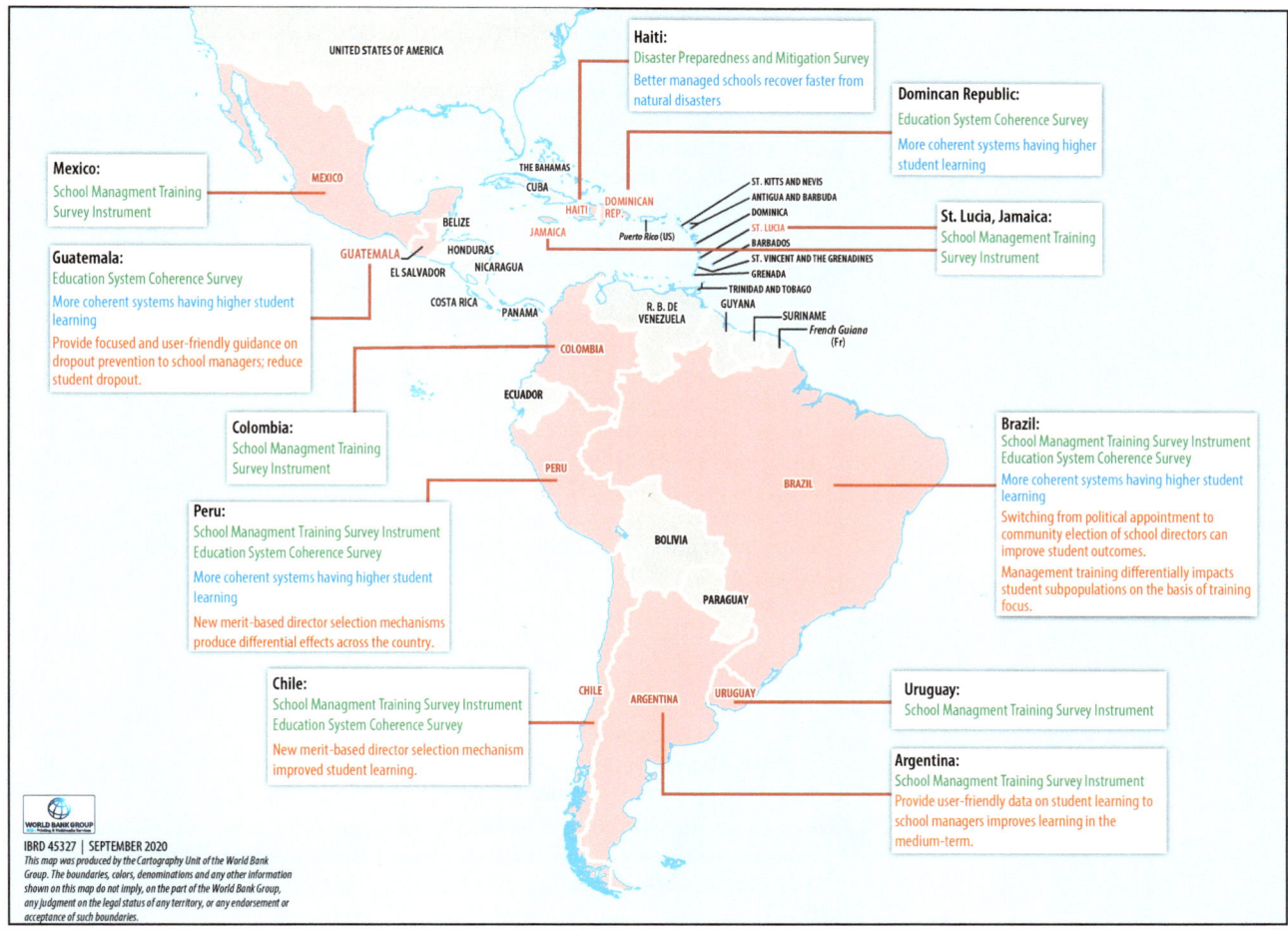

Source: World Bank.
Note: This figure summarizes the research presented throughout this study and is color coded as follows: measures of management (described in chapter 2, in green); evidence on how management matters for student outcomes (described in chapter 3, in blue); evidence on how to improve education management (described in chapter 4, in orange).

NOTES

1. For example, Hanushek and Woessmann (2015) show that average differences in international math and science test scores across countries can largely explain the drastically different GDP per capita growth trajectories of developing countries over the past 50 years. The authors use multiple specifications to test these relationships, including average test scores throughout the period regressed on average growth, average test scores in the first two decades regressed on growth in the subsequent two decades, and changes in test scores regressed on subsequent changes in growth rates for Latin American and East Asian countries.
2. In the lexicon of Banerjee and others (2017) on challenges to moving from proof-of-concept to implementing at scale, management plays a central role in two of the six challenges the authors discuss: randomization/site-selection bias and piloting bias.

3. Starting from the "accountability triangle" of the 2004 *World Development Report*, conceptual models of education as a service delivery system have focused on a similar set of factors, including the "3 As" model of autonomy, accountability, and assessment (Demas and Arcia 2015); accountability through autonomy, information, and incentives (Bruns, Filmer, and Patrinos 2011); and autonomy, accountability, and competition (Woessmann 2016).
4. More broadly, the substantial literature on public sector reform in developing countries has largely focused on form rather than function and rarely measures actual service delivery outcomes (Goldfinch, DeRouen, and Pospieszna 2012).
5. Many of these reforms were not explicitly designed to improve student learning but rather to expand access to schooling at relatively low cost. To the extent that the resulting schools produce learning on par with the rest of the public system, there is a strong argument that these reforms have efficiently met their primary objective.
6. In another recent example, Bergbauer, Hanushek, and Woessmann (2018) investigate how specific features of assessment systems correlate with student achievement across countries at different performance levels.
7. The Chilean experience has been extensively studied, and many of the recent studies are cited in Murnane et al. 2017.
8. This index was developed by Leaver, Lemos, and Scur (2019) using the PISA 2012 school questionnaire and is described in chapter 2.
9. Given the region's relatively weak global performance, the regional frontier may be an underestimate of potential productivity at a given input level. In addition, the index of management practices from PISA may have measurement error, as explained in Leaver, Lemos, and Scur (2019).

REFERENCES

Adelman, Melissa, and Miguel Székely. 2016. "School Dropout in Central America: An Overview of Trends, Causes, Consequences, and Promising Interventions." Policy Research Working Paper 7561, World Bank, Washington, DC.

Agasisti, Tommaso, and Pablo Zoido. 2018. "Comparing the Efficiency of Schools through International Benchmarking: Results from and Empirical Analysis of OECD PISA 2012 Data." *Educational Researcher* 20 (10): 1–11.

Angrist, Joshua, Parag Pathak, and Christopher Walters. 2013. "Explaining Charter School Effectiveness." *American Economic Journal: Applied Economics* 5 (4): 1–27.

Banerjee, Abhijit, Rukmini Banerji, James Berry, Esther Duflo, Harini Kannan, Shobhini Mukerji, Marc Shotland, and Michael Walton. 2017. "From Proof of Concept to Scalable Policies: Challenges and Solutions, with an Application." *Journal of Economic Perspectives* 31 (4): 73–102.

Barrera-Osorio, Felipe, Tazeen Fasih, Harry Anthony Patrinos, and Lucrecia Santibañez. 2009. *Decentralized Decision-Making in Schools. The Theory and Evidence on School-Based Management*. Directions in Development Series. Washington, DC: World Bank.

Bassi, Marina, Matias Busso, and Juan Sebastian Muñoz. 2015. "Enrollment, Graduation, and Dropout Rates in Latin America: Is the Glass Half Empty or Half Full?" *Economía Journal of the Latin American and Caribbean Economic Association—LACEA* Fall 2015: 113–56.

Bergbauer, Annika, Eric Hanushek, and Ludger Woessmann. 2018. "Testing." NBER Working Paper 24836, National Bureau of Economic Research, Cambridge, MA.

Bloom, Nicholas, Benn Eifert, Aprajit Mahajan, David McKenzie, and John Roberts. 2013. "Does Management Matter? Evidence from India." *The Quarterly Journal of Economics* 128 (1): 1–51.

Bloom, Nicholas, Renata Lemos, Raffaella Sadun, and John Van Reenen. 2015. "Does Management Matter in Schools?" *The Economic Journal* 125 (584): 647–74.

Bloom, Nicholas, Aprajit Mahajan, David McKenzie, and John Roberts. 2020. "Do Management Interventions Last? Evidence from India." *American Economic Journal: Applied Economics* 12 (2): 198–219.

Bloom, Nicholas, Raffaella Sadun, and John Van Reenen. 2017. "Management as a Technology?" NBER Working Paper 22327, National Bureau of Economic Research, Cambridge, MA.

Bold, Tessa, Deon Filmer, Gayle Martin, Ezequiel Molina, Christophe Rockmore, Brian Stacy, Jakob Svensson, and Waly Wane. 2017. "What Do Teachers Know and Do? Does It Matter? Evidence from Primary Schools in Africa." Policy Research Working Paper 7956, World Bank, Washington, DC.

Bruhn, Miriam, Dean Karlan, and Antoinette Schoar. 2018. "The Impact of Consulting Services on Small and Medium Enterprises: Evidence from a Randomized Trial in Mexico." *Journal of Political Economy* 126 (2): 635–87.

Bruns, Barbara, Deon Filmer, and Harry Patrinos. 2011. *Making Schools Work. New Evidence on Accountability Reforms*. Human Development Perspectives. Washington, DC: World Bank.

de la Torre, Augusto, Alain Ize, and Samuel Pienknagura. 2015. *Latin America Treads a Narrow Path to Growth: LAC Semiannual Report, April 2015*. Washington, DC: World Bank.

Demas, Angela, and Gustavo Arcia. 2015. "What Matters Most for School Autonomy and Accountability: A Framework Paper." Systems Approach for Better Education Results (SABER) Working Paper Series Number 9. World Bank.

Di Gropello, Emanuela. 2006. "A Comparative Analysis of School-Based Management in Central America." World Bank Working Paper No. 72. Washington, DC: World Bank.

Dobbie, Will, and Roland G. Fryer Jr. 2013. "Getting Beneath the Veil of Effective Schools: Evidence from New York City." *American Economic Journal: Applied Economics* 5: 28–60.

Evans, David and Anna Popova. 2016. "What Really Works to Improve Learning in Developing Countries? An Analysis of Divergent Findings in Systematic Reviews." *World Bank Research Observer* 31 (2): 242–70.

Ferreira, Francisco, Julián Messina, Jamele Rigolini, Luis Felipe López-Calva, María Ana Lugo, and Renos Vakis. 2013. *Economic Mobility and the Rise of the Latin American Middle Class*. Washington, DC: World Bank

Ganimian, Alejandro, and Richard Murnane. 2016. "Improving Educational Outcomes in Developing Countries: Lessons from Rigorous Evaluations." *Review of Educational Research* 86 (3): 719–55.

Gibbons, Robert, and John Roberts. 2013. *The Handbook of Organizational Economics*. Princeton, NJ: Princeton University Press.

Giorcelli, Michela. 2019. "The Long-Term Effects of Management and Technology Transfer." *American Economic Review* 109 (1): 121–55.

Glewwe, Paul, and Karthik Muralidharan. 2016. "Improving School Education Outcomes in Developing Countries: Evidence, Knowledge Gaps, and Policy Implications." In *Handbook of the Economics of Education*, edited by E. A. Hanushek, S. Machin, and L. Woessmann (vol. 5), 653–743. North Holland, Amsterdam.

Goldfinch, Shaun, Karl DeRouen, and Paulina Pospieszna. 2012. "Flying Blind? Evidence for Good Governance Public Management Reform Agendas, Implementations and Outcomes in Low Income Countries." *Public Administration and Development* 33 (1): 50–61.

González-Velosa, Carolina, David Rosas, and Roberto Flores. 2016. "On-the-Job Training in Latin America and the Caribbean: Recent Evidence." In *Firm Innovation and Productivity in Latin America and the Caribbean: The Engine of Economic Development*, edited by Matteo Grazzi and Carlo Pietrobelli, 137–66. Washington, DC: Inter-American Development Bank; New York: Springer Nature.

Hanushek, Eric, and Ludger Woessmann. 2012a. "Do Better Schools Lead to More Growth? Cognitive Skills, Economic Outcomes, and Causation." *Journal of Economic Growth* 17 (4): 267–321.

Hanushek, Eric, and Ludger Woessmann. 2012b. "Schooling, Educational Achievement, and the Latin American Growth Puzzle." *Journal of Development Economics*. 99 (2): 497–512.

Hanushek, Eric, Susanne Link, and Ludger Woessmann. 2013. "Does School Autonomy Make Sense Everywhere? Panel Estimates from PISA." *Journal of Development Economics* 104: 212–232.

Hanushek, Eric, and Ludger Woessmann. 2015. *The Knowledge Capital of Nations: Education and the Economics of Growth*. Cambridge: MIT Press.

Harris, Alma, and Michelle Jones. 2020. "COVID 19—School Leadership in Disruptive Times." *School Leadership & Management* 40 (4): 243–47.

Higuchi, Yuki, Edwin Mhede, and Tetsushi Sonobe. 2016. "Short- and Longer-Run Impacts of Management Training: An Experiment in Tanzania." *World Development* 114: 120–26.

Leaver, Clare, Renata Lemos, and Daniela Scur. 2019. "Measuring and Explaining Management in Schools: New Approaches Using Public Data." Policy Research Working Paper 9053, World Bank, Washington, DC.

McEwan, Patrick. 2015. "Improving Learning in Primary Schools of Developing Countries: A Meta-Analysis of Randomized Experiments." *Review of Educational Research* 85 (3): 353–94.

Murnane, Richard, Marcus Waldman, John Willett, Maria Soledad Bos, and Emiliana Vegas. 2017. "The Consequences of Educational Voucher Reform in Chile." NBER Working Paper 23550, National Bureau of Economic Research, Cambridge, MA.

Pritchett, Lant. 2015. "Creating Education Systems Coherent for Learning Outcomes: Making the Transition from Schooling to Learning." RISE Working Paper 15/005." Oxford: Research on Improving Systems of Education (RISE).

Székely, Miguel, and Jonathan Karver. 2021. "Youth Out of School and Out of Work in Latin America: A Cohort Approach." *International Journal of Educational Development* 80: 102294.

Végh, Carlos, Guillermo Vuletin, Daniel Riera-Crichton, Diego Friedheim, Luis Morano, and José Andrée Camarena. 2018. *Fiscal Adjustment in Latin America and the Caribbean: Short-Run Pain, Long-Run Gain? LAC Semiannual Report, April 2018*. Washington, DC: World Bank.

WISE (World Innovation Summit for Education). 2020. Education Disrupted, Education Reimagined: Responses from Education's Frontline during the COVID-19 Pandemic and Beyond. https://www.wise-qatar.org/special-edition-e-book-education-disrupted-education-reimagined/.

Woessmann, Ludger. 2016. "The Importance of School Systems: Evidence from International Differences in Student Achievement." *Journal of Economic Perspectives* 30 (3): 3–32.)

World Bank. 2013. *World Development Report 2014: Risk and Opportunity—Managing Risk for Development*. Washington, DC: World Bank.

World Bank. 2018. *World Development Report 2018: Learning to Realize Education's Promise*. Washington, DC: World Bank.

World Bank. 2020a. *The Economy in the Time of Covid-19. LAC Semiannual Report: April 2020*. Washington, DC: World Bank.

World Bank. 2020b. *The COVID-19 Pandemic: Shocks to Education and Policy Responses*. Washington, DC: World Bank.

World Bank. Forthcoming. *Study to Explore the Perceived Effectiveness of Remote Learning*.

2 Managers, Structures, and Practices

ADVANCES IN MEASURING EDUCATION MANAGEMENT

In education research, the relationship between management, administration, and leadership, and their relative importance, remain the subject of debate (Bush 2019; Connolly, James, and Fertig 2019). For the purposes of this study, we use the term *management*, though we consider research and data that use these different terms.

Management can perhaps be most readily conceptualized as the practices used to coordinate resources to achieve a common goal, such as allocating tasks and monitoring their completion, setting the pace of work, and administering both human and physical resources. These practices help determine how critical inputs for education service delivery, from teachers to textbooks to infrastructure, come together in schools and classrooms. Two of the most proximate determinants of management practices are managers themselves (their skills, motivation, experience, and demographics) and the organizational structures that are in place to manage schools and education systems (that is, the rules and available resources), which in turn are shaped by the political, socioeconomic, and broader characteristics of any given context. Throughout this study, we focus specifically on practices, managers, and organizational structures but recognize the need for future research that considers their interaction with political and socioeconomic factors.

To organize and simplify the broad concept of education management, we focus primarily on public education systems and distinguish between three levels of management: management of individual schools, management of the middle layers (defined units such as a local administrative district or a central technical unit), and management of an education system as a whole (such as a basic education ministry). At each level, effective management of day-to-day activities as well as shocks can affect student outcomes through multiple channels.

This chapter first describes the proximate determinants of management practices—the managers and organizational structures in place across education systems in Latin America and the Caribbean (LAC)—using a range of existing and newly collected data. We focus on school directors and other school-level managers, given the importance of this level for student outcomes and the availability of information. We then discuss recent advances in the measurement of management practices in education. In particular, we describe instruments developed within the past several years (including several developed as part of research conducted for this study) to quantitatively measure the quality of management practices in schools and in middle layers, as well as to discuss the organizational structures of education systems.

WHO THE MANAGERS ARE IN LAC'S PUBLIC SCHOOLS

Public systems of basic education across LAC vary in their allocation of authority—from centralized systems common in the smaller countries of the Caribbean and Central America, to federated systems like Mexico's and Argentina's, to highly decentralized systems like Brazil's. Yet across this diversity of structures, two key managerial roles at the school level are present in the majority of LAC countries: school director (or school principal or head teacher) and school management committee (or school board or school council). With some exceptions, countries across LAC have not fully "professionalized" their school director workforce and rely on appointing teachers to fill the role without specific performance criteria, specialized training, or career paths. At the same time, school management committees have played a central role in many countries' efforts to strengthen school quality, with mixed results. In this section, we synthesize what we know about both directors and management committees in the region using the data now available thanks to growing participation of the region in international standardized assessments. Understanding the people who serve as managers—their skills, their activities, and the opportunities they are given to improve their work—is a critical part of improving management in education.

School directors

To establish what is known about primary public school directors, we focus on three questions. Who becomes a school director in LAC? What is a director's role? And what are the characteristics of the job? To answer these questions, we draw from the supplemental questionnaires of the 2013 Third Regional and Comparative Explanatory Study (TERCE) and the 2013 Teaching and Learning International Survey (TALIS); a survey conducted as a follow-up to Adelman and others (forthcoming) in four LAC countries; government documentation; and existing research. These questionnaires generate comparable data across countries based on self-reported information from school directors themselves; the questionnaires also can be used to some extent to assess the managerial realities in schools compared with formal policies.[1]

Countries vary in the requirements they place on candidates for public school director positions and on the selection methods they use. Some countries have relatively well-developed competitive selection mechanisms, such as Argentina and Uruguay, and some have specific educational requirements beyond teaching degrees, such as Nicaragua and Peru.[2] Across LAC, multiple selection methods coexist within countries, and the most common type of selection mechanism is merit-based competition, followed closely by appointment by the authorities (figure 2.1). Directors' educational levels also vary, both within and across countries (figure 2.2). In some countries, including Guatemala, Nicaragua, and

FIGURE 2.1

Coexistence of multiple selection methods for public school directors, including merit-based competition and appointment by authorities, within Latin American and Caribbean countries

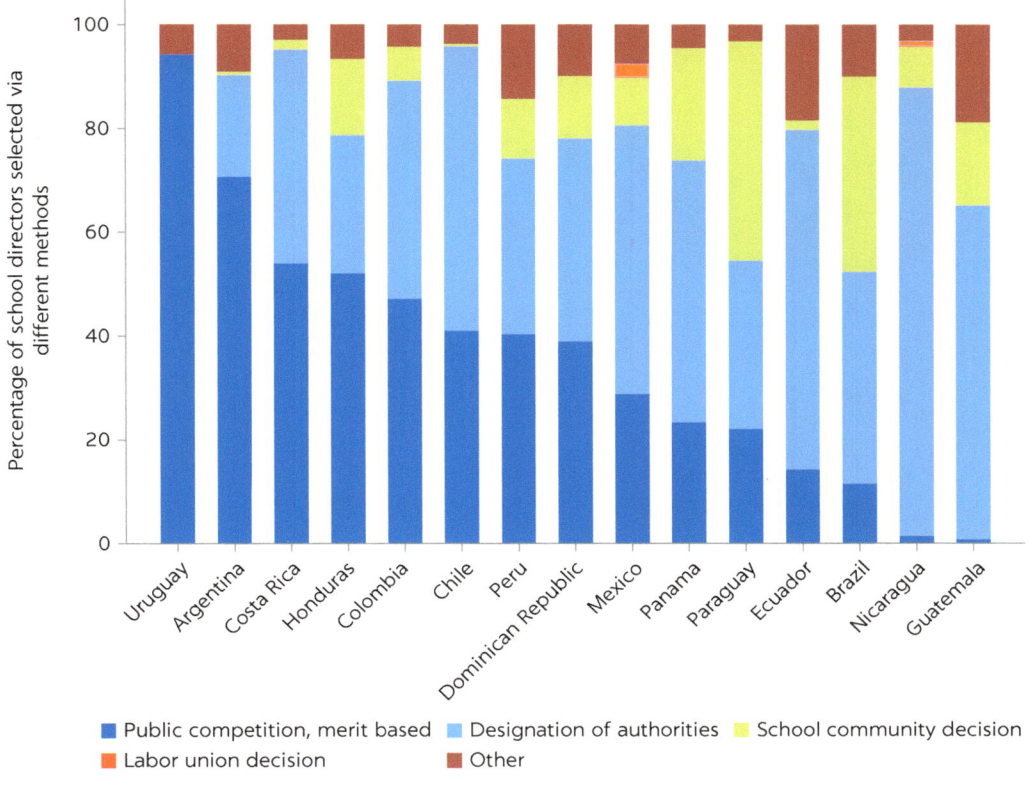

Source: World Bank.
Note: This figure shows the percentage of public primary school directors who reported obtaining their post through each selection method, using data from the 2013 TERCE. School weights are used to compute country-level statistics. The underlying question is *How did you obtain your position as director at this school?*, and possible answers are public competition, school community designation, designation by educational or municipal authorities, school promoters or owners decision, labor union decision, and other. School community and school owner answers are combined under "school community."

Honduras, a sizable percentage of school directors have a secondary or postsecondary nonuniversity education, while in others, such as Colombia and Chile, nearly all directors are university graduates.

Although directors are drawn almost exclusively from the stock of teachers, there is at least a 20-point gap in the percentage of female directors compared with female teachers in eight of the 15 countries participating in TERCE (figure 2.3). This dearth of female leaders is found in many sectors and countries and points to the need to carefully examine the countries' mechanisms for developing and selecting school directors, with consideration of the biases, discriminatory practices, or other challenges that may play a role (Gipson and others 2017; Martínez, Molina-López, and Mateos de Cabo 2020). Across most of the LAC countries with available data, primary school directors start in their positions relatively young, between 30 and 40 years of age, and remain directors for a long time, with current directors having, on average, 5 to 15 years of experience in the role (figure 2.4).

FIGURE 2.2
Substantial variation in the education level of public school directors across Latin American and Caribbean countries

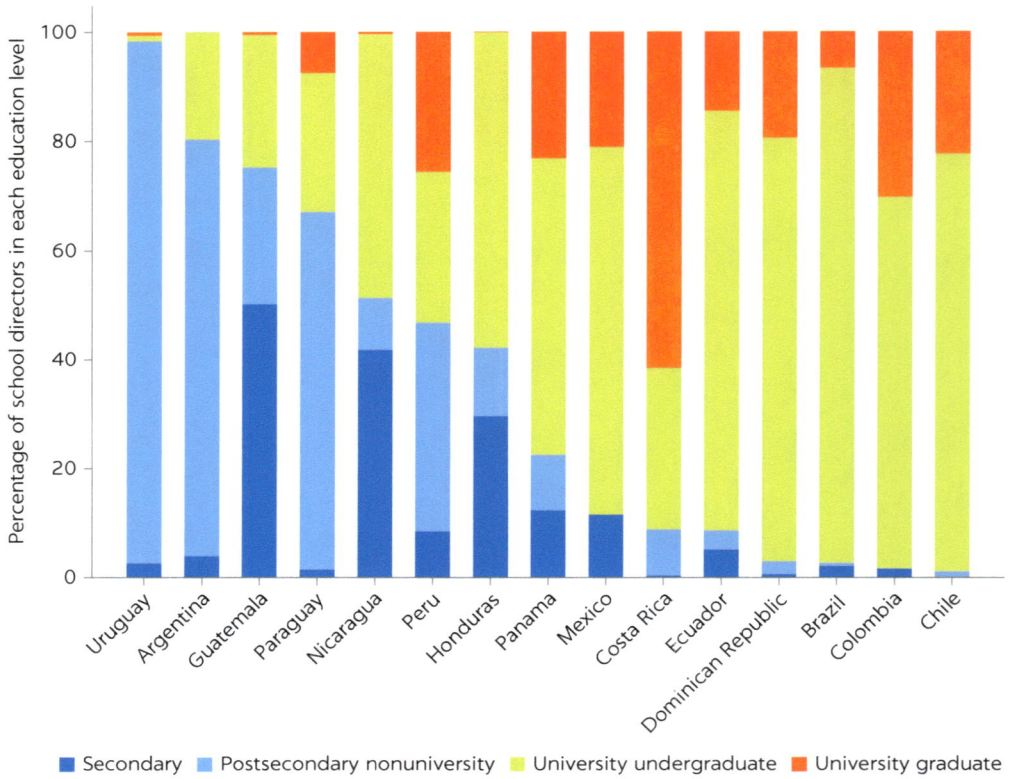

Source: World Bank.
Note: This figure shows the percentage of public primary school directors who have completed each education level: secondary, postsecondary nonuniversity, university undergraduate, and university graduate (master's and doctoral degrees) using data from the 2013 TERCE. School weights are used to compute country-level statistics.

School-based management and school management committees

In LAC, over 60 percent of directors in 11 of the 15 countries that participated in the TERCE assessment report the existence of a school management committee (SMC) or similar entity for their school (figure 2.5). Initiatives across the region over the past several decades have created or devolved responsibilities to such entities. The underlying hypothesis of the initiatives is that giving local school leaders and parents more influence and decision-making authority can improve communication, monitoring, transparency, and accountability, thereby making schools more responsive to student needs and improving the quality of the service (Bruns, Filmer, and Patrinos 2011; World Bank 2007). Each program is shaped by the objectives of the reformers and the broader national policy and social context in which it is created, but there are two key dimensions that help define SMCs: to whom the decision-making authority devolves (composition), and the extent of autonomy devolved (responsibilities).

In nearly all countries, the composition of SMCs is mandated in regulations and usually consists of a combination of directors, teachers, parents, sometimes

FIGURE 2.3
Public school directors skew male when compared to teachers across Latin American and Caribbean countries

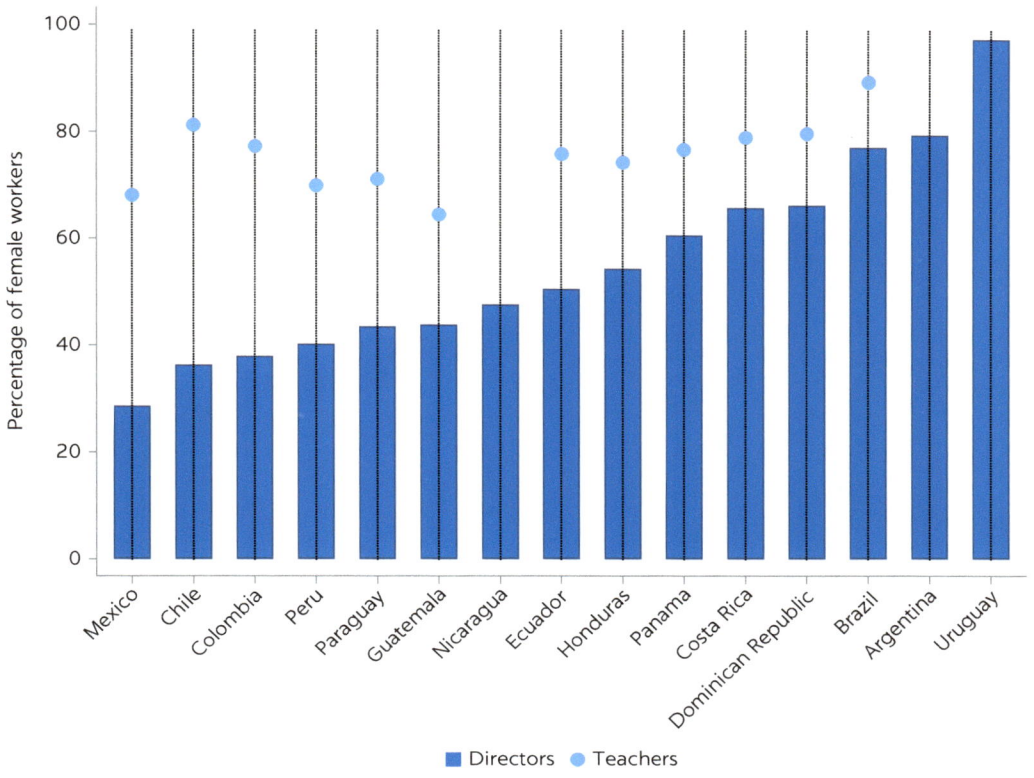

Source: World Bank.
Note: This figure shows the percentage of public sector female workers for two categories of workers in the education sector—primary school directors and teachers— using data from the 2013 TERCE. The bars show the percentage of female directors relative to the total number of directors, whereas the dot shows the percentage of female teachers relative to the total number of teachers. Teacher weights are used to compute school-level statistics, followed by school weights to compute country-level statistics. Data for teachers is not available for Nicaragua, Argentina, and Uruguay.

students, and other school community members (Carr-Hill, 2017). In most cases, parents are de jure in the majority, with the director or head teacher acting as the chair or secretary. Many schools also have parent associations that may or may not be formally involved in the SMC (Santibañez, Abreu-Lastra, and O'Donoghue 2014).

Areas of authority or roles assigned to SMCs vary substantially across countries and can range from infrastructure improvement to budget allocation to hiring and firing of teachers. Depending on the responsibilities devolved, SMCs can be classified as (a) strong, in which the committee has almost full control of schools, or a high degree of autonomy over staffing and budgets; (b) intermediate, in which SMCs have authority to set curricula but limited autonomy regarding resources; and (c) weak, in which SMCs are established but mainly in an advisory role (Barrera-Osorio and others 2009; Bruns, Filmer, and Patrinos 2011).

Despite the popularity of SMCs, and some evidence that they and other school-based management reforms have played an important role, their impacts on student outcomes are mixed and depend on context and the extent of complementary measures. For example, a comparative analysis of Central America's

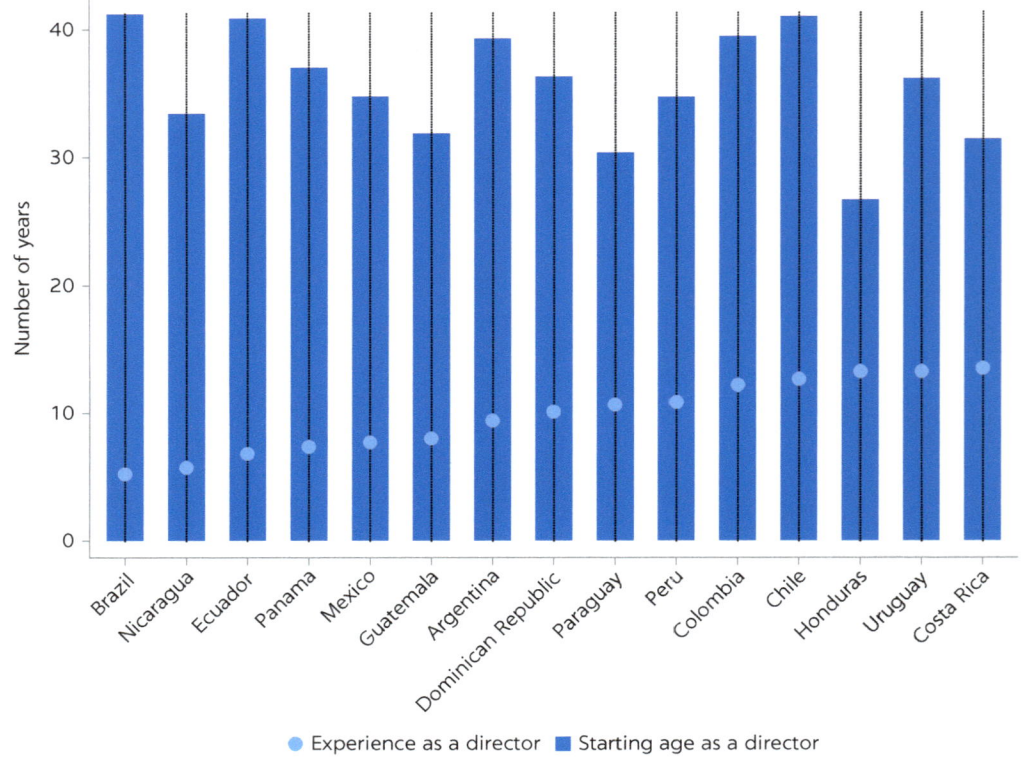

FIGURE 2.4

Public school directors start at a young age and stay in the post for several years in many Latin American and Caribbean countries

● Experience as a director ■ Starting age as a director

Source: World Bank.
Note: This figure shows the average starting age and the number of years of experience as a public primary school director, using data from the 2013 TERCE. The bar shows the starting age, whereas the dot shows the years of experience. School weights are used to compute country-level statistics.

school-based management models finds that the approach succeeded in expanding access to education in rural areas through more efficient use of scarce resources, with student achievement outcomes on par with traditional schools (Di Gropello 2006). However, results from a number of randomized evaluations are mixed and point to the importance of program elements that include loosening binding constraints in a given context to affect student achievement. For example, supplemental cash grants to school councils led to higher test scores in Mexico, but in The Gambia such grants needed to be coupled with capacity building to have an impact (and then only for communities with higher baseline capacity). And in Indonesia neither grants nor training had effects on student learning, but linking school councils to local authorities and instituting more representative elections did (Blimpo, Evans, and Lahire 2015; Pradhan and others 2014; Santibañez, Abreu-Lastra, and O'Donoghue 2014). One possible shortcoming of randomized evaluations is the usually short horizon for measuring impacts, because communities may need time to learn how to effectively implement school management (Borman and others 2003). However, even among studies that allowed at least eight years before measuring the effects of school-based management interventions on test scores, results are mixed,

FIGURE 2.5

Many public school directors are supported by school councils or management committees across Latin American and Caribbean countries

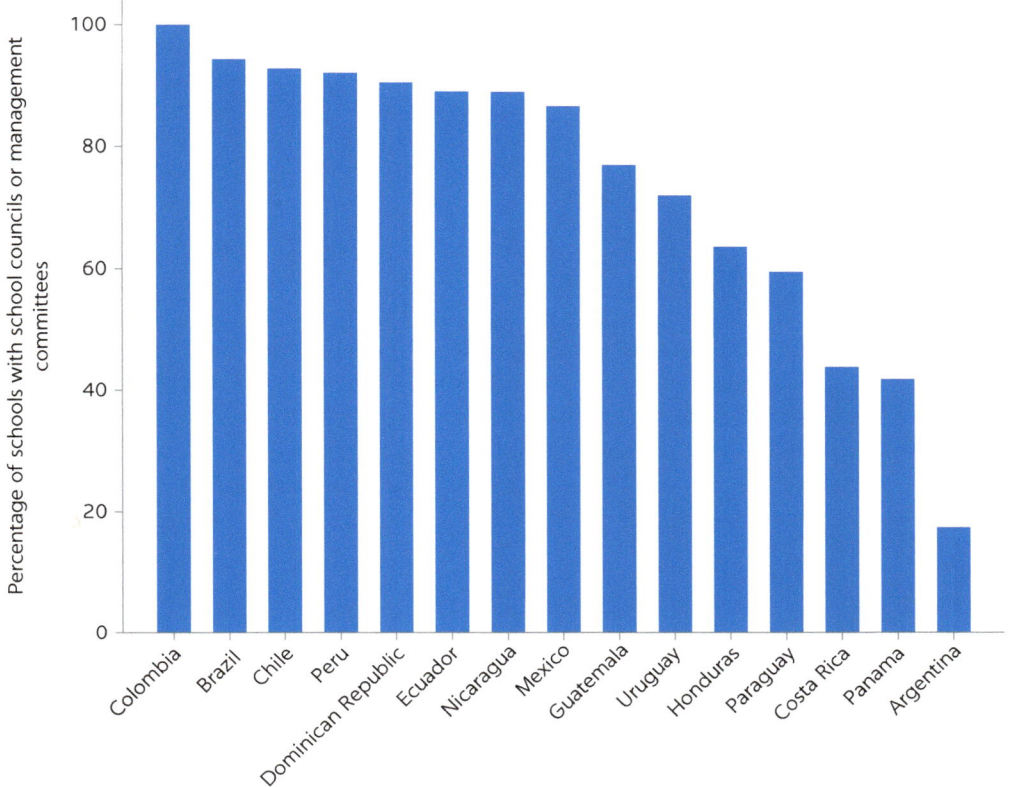

Source: World Bank.
Note: This figure shows the percentage of public primary school directors reporting to work with a school council or management committee, using data from the 2013 TERCE. School weights are used to compute country-level statistics.

with no effects of reform in Brazil after 11 years, but positive impacts in Nicaragua and Mexico (Bruns, Filmer, and Patrinos 2011; López-Calva and Espinosa 2006; Paes de Barros and Mendonça 1998; World Bank 2018).

Other managerial roles in schools

Beyond directors and school management committees, other leadership positions exist in some schools in some countries. The existence of these positions has been less systematically documented, but a small survey about the school team composition in four LAC countries collected by Adelman and others (forthcoming) illustrate several points. First, important differences in the structure of school management across countries are likely to affect how career frameworks for directors are developed and implemented. For example, 97 percent of Brazilian directors in the survey report that the role of pedagogical coordinator formally exists at their school and that this person holds primary responsibility for supervising teaching. Only 9 percent of Peruvian directors in the survey report the existence of this role. Second, the existence of additional management roles, including pedagogical coordinator, vice principal, or administrative coordinator, is correlated with school size, and directors in smaller schools are more likely to report holding primary responsibility in different areas. Directors in small schools (the bottom quintile in terms of student population) also report spending over 20 percent of their time teaching classes, compared with less than 5 percent spent by directors of schools in the top quintile. This suggests that for small schools, where directors are playing multiple roles, strengthening the management layer above the school level could be a particularly important lever for improving outcomes.

ORGANIZATIONAL STRUCTURES TO MANAGE LAC'S SCHOOLS AND EDUCATION SYSTEMS

The second proximate determinant of management practices that we consider is organizational structures, including the rules and resources that shape the context in which managers work. Relatively limited evidence on these aspects is available in existing datasets, so this section focuses on school directors' allocated responsibilities and career structures, based on existing data, as well as the characteristics of in-service training programs available to them, based on newly collected data from the region.

Responsibilities and career structures

Responsibilities of school directors across LAC are numerous and broad, running from administration to community engagement, which is also the case in many OECD countries (Pont, Nusche, and Moorman 2008). Between 15 percent and 88 percent of primary school directors across countries in LAC report that they also have teaching responsibilities at their school and are therefore playing at least two roles simultaneously, according to the 2013 TERCE assessment. Despite having broad responsibilities, directors have limited autonomy in actual decision-making on budget and curricular management, and virtually no autonomy in personnel management (figure 2.6).[3] These self-reports from 2015 PISA are supported by Adelman and others (forthcoming), who find that across Brazil, the Dominican Republic, Guatemala, and Peru, school directors are formally allocated responsibility for a minority of core education management tasks, and that their allocated tasks are largely confined to reporting their school data and needs to higher level authorities. These results highlight that public school directors are in many cases managing their teachers without formal authority and must use practices other than high-powered personnel management practices to affect the quality of teachers' work (a discussion we return to in chapter 3).

Regarding the profession or career of school director, some countries have well-defined frameworks and standards, such as Chile, Colombia, Jamaica, Mexico, and Peru, but regular, consequential performance evaluation based on such standards is not yet a reality in most LAC countries, with the exception of Colombia (Flessa and others 2018; Nannyonjo 2017). Even across the OECD countries, where many have well-developed standards, creating reliable assessment tools remains a challenge (Pont, Nusche, and Moorman 2008). Directors in many countries hold indefinite appointments (figure 2.7), and financial incentives

FIGURE 2.6

Public school directors have more decision-making autonomy over practices directly affecting students than over personnel practices in most Latin American and Caribbean countries

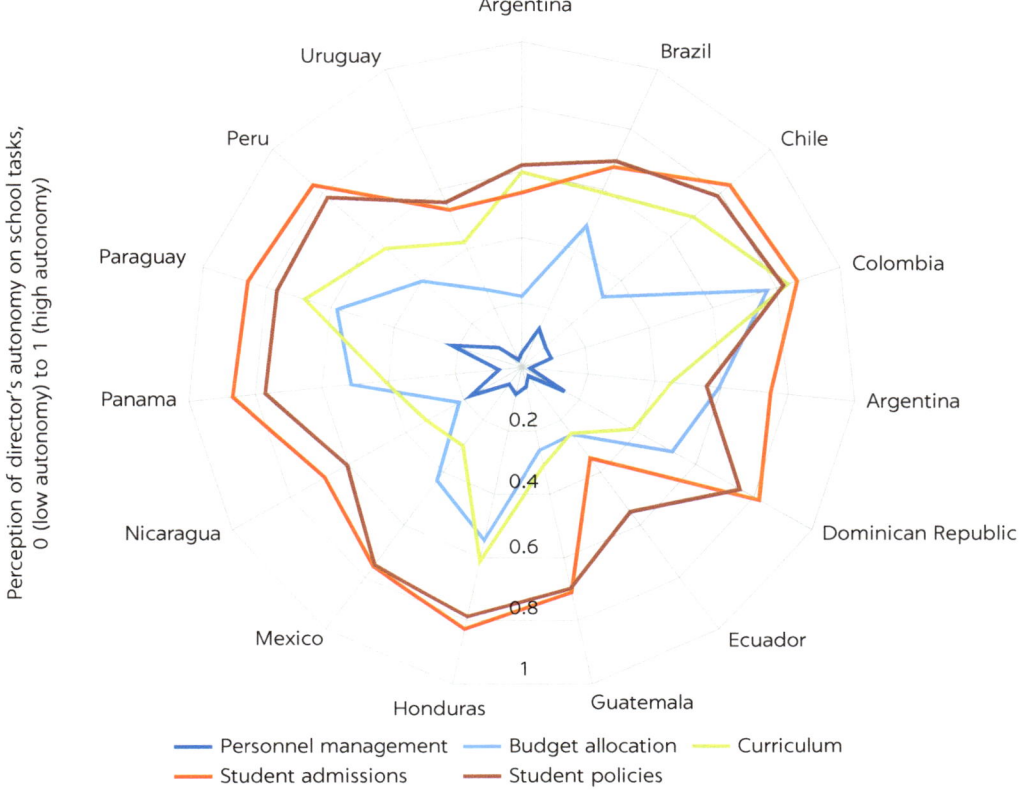

Source: World Bank.
Note: The figure shows the self-reported level of autonomy public primary school directors have over five different dimensions (budget, curriculum, student admissions, student policies, and personnel management), using data from the 2013 TERCE. School weights are used to compute country-level statistics. A value of 0 indicates that directors in the country on average self-report having no role for decision-making for activities in the area. A value of 1 indicates that directors in the country on average self-report having primary responsibility in decision-making for activities in that area.

and clearly defined opportunities for upward mobility are rare. Motivating performance in these contexts is a challenging task, a topic that will be returned to in chapter 4 (Weinstein and Hernández 2016). Regarding training, while the majority of directors across LAC hold postsecondary degrees, more countries are developing induction and in-service training specifically for school directors. However, the characteristics of these programs and their impacts on directors' subsequent performance has not been well studied (Weinstein, Azar, and Flessa 2018).

Management training

Given the dearth of information on the type of management training available to school directors, we collected data from 13 government-supported school management training programs in nine countries in Latin America and the

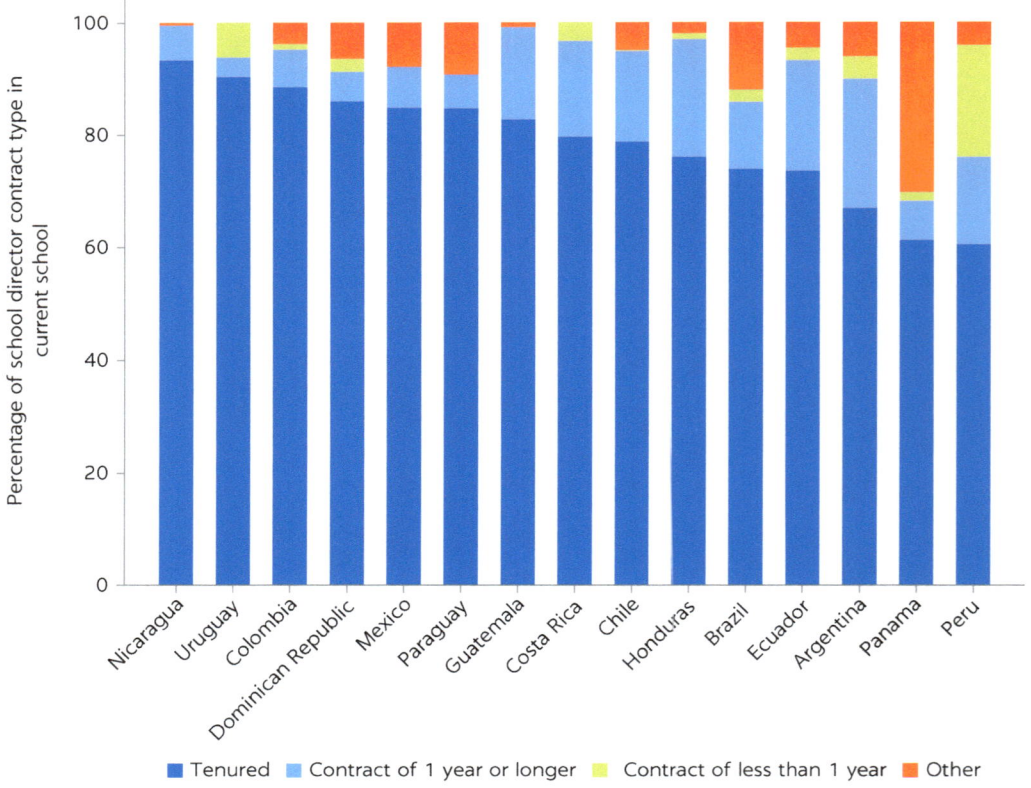

FIGURE 2.7

The majority of public school directors have indefinite contracts with their schools across Latin American and Caribbean countries

Source: World Bank.
Note: This figure shows the percentage of public primary school directors reporting their type of contract (labor relations), using data from the 2013 TERCE. School weights are used to compute country-level statistics.

Caribbean—Argentina, Brazil, Chile, Colombia, Jamaica, Mexico, Peru, St. Lucia, and Uruguay. We followed the work of Popova and others (2018) by slightly adapting their In-Service Teacher Training Survey Instrument to create a School Management Training Survey Instrument (SMTSI) to survey training program managers about the characteristics of their programs.

Survey questions in the SMTSI follow the defining attributes of professional development programs identified by Popova and others (2018): (a) program organization, including implementation characteristics, program design and targeting, and professional implications and incentives; (b) program content, asking which school management practices used in the World Management Survey are taught during the program (Bloom and others 2015); and (c) program delivery, including type of activities used during core delivery and postprogram monitoring, duration and distribution of time across different delivery modalities, and trainer profile.

To understand which specific program attributes are important features of teacher training programs, Popova and others (2018) correlated program characteristics with outcomes of students whose teachers participated in the program. Several characteristics associated with higher student learning gains stand out as likely to also be relevant for school management training programs, including: (a) clear incentives to participate in the program, such as promotion or salary implications; (b) a specific subject focus; (c) a strong practice component, with teachers practicing delivering lessons during the training; (d) at least an initial face-to-face interaction during training; and (e) mentoring through follow-up visits after the training has ended (an additional characteristic perceived by surveyed program managers as important). The following overview of the 13 school management training programs surveyed focuses on these important characteristics.

Program organization

Implementation: Over 60 percent of the school management training programs were established after 2015 (the oldest was 2007), suggesting that this type of training at large scale is relatively new. The majority of programs are designed (93 percent) and implemented (100 percent) with the help of nongovernmental organizations, and most programs (77 percent) are offered at the national level or across multiple states or regions.[4]

Diagnosis: Only a few respondents indicated that their program's design was based on a formal diagnostic tool or evaluation of manager skills (31 percent), of student learning (31 percent), or of teacher skills (15 percent). The remainder of respondents indicated that the program's design had been either based on an informal diagnostic or not based on any diagnostic (figure 2.8, panel a). In fact, only two programs (15 percent) reported that their design was based on a formal evaluation of all three categories, suggesting that the large majority of programs surveyed are not taking into consideration existing skills and performance to ensure that they are tailored and relevant to the target population.

Professional implications: Posttraining evaluation exists in 85 percent of the programs surveyed. However, only 61 percent of respondents indicated that it is possible to fail the evaluation, and the percentage of managers failing the evaluation is still extremely low for these programs (below 1 percent in all but two responses). Respondents also reported whether there are positive consequences of passing the evaluation for managers (figure 2.8, panel b). Positive consequences for passing the training program evaluation are more common than negative consequences for failing. Public status and recognition (61 percent of training programs) and certification (54 percent) are positive consequences for passing the evaluation; yet only one program uses the results in promotion decisions. Implications of failing the training program are rare, with only one program withholding certification and no program using the evaluation results in promotion decisions. None of the respondents surveyed indicated any consequence, positive or negative, in which the results of the evaluation affected salary decisions. Going back to the results in Popova and others (2018), professional implications, and more specifically promotion or salary implications, are identified as important features of teacher training programs, yet these characteristics are largely absent from the school management training programs surveyed.

And who is informed of the results of training evaluations? Although all programs indicated that the local education authority or ministry of education are informed of the results, only 61 percent of programs indicated that participating managers themselves receive the results of their evaluations.

FIGURE 2.8

Government-supported management training programs in selected Latin American and Caribbean countries are a good start but have substantial room for improvement in their organization, content, and delivery

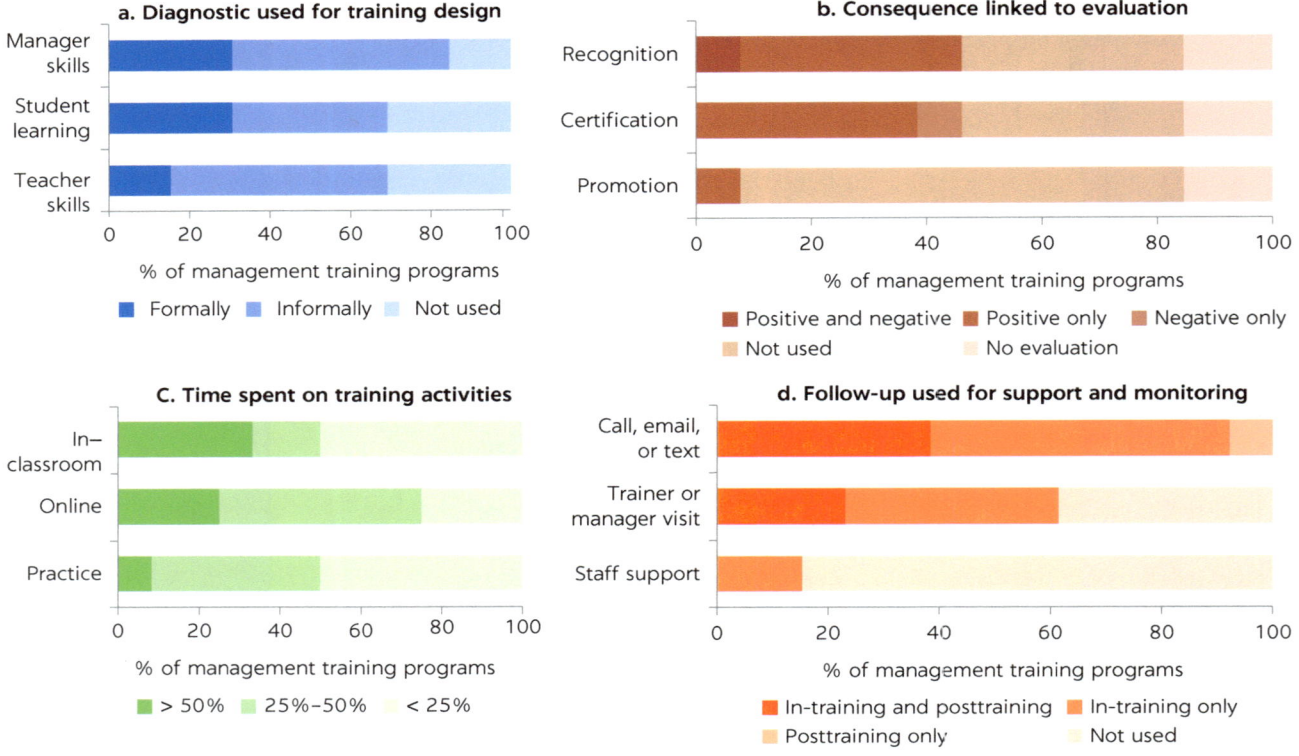

Source: World Bank.
Note: This figure shows the results of the School Management Training Survey with 13 large programs in Argentina, Brazil, Chile, Colombia, Jamaica, Mexico, Peru, Saint Lucia, and Uruguay. Panel a indicates whether programs were designed on the basis of a diagnostic or evaluation of student learning, teacher skills, or manager skills. Panel b indicates how much time managers spend on in-classroom, online, or practice activities. Panel c indicates whether the results of an end-of-training evaluation have any professional implications for managers, more specifically negative implications for failing the evaluation or positive implications for passing the evaluation. Panel d indicates what type of follow-up support is provided while the program is on course and after the program has ended.

Program content

Popova and others (2018) suggest that teacher training programs with a specific subject focus (as opposed to more general programs) are associated with higher learning gains. To understand the focus of school management training programs in LAC, we asked respondents to indicate whether the program content included activities on 25 management topics in five dimensions: operations management, performance monitoring, target setting, people management, and leadership. If they responded yes, we asked respondents to indicate whether these topics were included formally (mandatory) as part of the program or only as part of an informal discussion (and thus not necessarily mandatory).

The information provided shows that no program focuses specifically on a single management dimension. That is, most programs formally include topics across several dimensions: 92 percent of programs indicate that activities in operations management, performance monitoring, and people management are included, and 100 percent of programs indicate that activities in target setting and leadership are included.[5]

Training programs that offer general training on a broad range of management practices and topics can provide school directors with an overview of the types of practices they should be implementing. However, it is unlikely that topics can be covered in sufficient depth for school directors to master the necessary skills to adopt the practices effectively in their schools.

Program delivery

Time use: The structure of the management training varies substantially across programs, with the number of training weeks ranging from 2 to 80 (median of 20 weeks). The total number of hours of course delivery also varies considerably from 72 to 650 (median of 235). Regarding the division of training hours across different delivery methods, the median program indicates that managers spend 33 percent of their time in face-to-face (in-person) sessions, 41 percent of their time in online training, and 22 percent of their time in practice sessions. Popova and others (2018) suggest that at least an initial face-to-face session, as well as practice sessions, are important features associated with higher learning gains. The survey shows that face-to-face (in-person) training is the most common used in training for 33 percent of programs, while online is the most common for 25 percent of programs, and practical training is the most common for only 8 percent of the programs (that is, one program), suggesting that some but not all programs focus on face-to-face interactions and practical exercises (figure 2.8, panel c).

Type of activity during core delivery, follow-up, and monitoring: Respondents indicated that the most common type of activity carried out during core delivery of training program content is group work (54 percent). Respondents also indicated that the most common secondary type is group discussion (38 percent), followed closely by lectures (31 percent).

Regarding support and monitoring, 77 percent, 62 percent, and 54 percent of programs provide support through email, phone calls, and text messages, respectively, while participants are still in the course. After the training program ends, these numbers fall to 46 percent, 23 percent, and 23 percent, respectively (figure 2.8, panel d).[6] Popova and others (2018) indicate that posttraining follow-up and monitoring were perceived by teacher training program managers as important features of their programs. Strong follow-up in school management training programs may also help managers absorb concepts learned during training and effectively implement best practices in their schools. Yet 46 percent of all programs report not having any type of follow-up or monitoring after the training program has ended.

THE SUPPLY AND QUALITY OF EDUCATION MANAGEMENT PRACTICES IN LAC

Given the breadth and qualitative nature of management practices, objectively and consistently measuring such practices in schools is a challenge. Three types of recently developed instruments offer new tools for measuring the supply of day-to-day school management, the quality of this management, and the management of shocks to schools.

Allocation of time across school management activities

Several instruments, primarily developed in the United States, provide quantitative measures of individual school directors' own total labor supply and allocation of time to different managerial activities. For example, Spillane and Hunt (2010) use an experience sampling methodology that periodically prompts directors to self-report their activities throughout the day, and another method uses a time-use instrument completed by observers who shadow directors throughout their day (Horng, Klasik, and Loeb 2010). The latter instrument categorizes school directors' job tasks into six categories—administration, organization management, day-to-day instruction, instructional program, internal relations, and external relations—that are further subdivided into 43 tasks. Using this categorization, trained observers followed (shadowed) secondary school directors in the United States and recorded the task directors were engaged in, with whom, and where every few minutes throughout one day. Grissom, Loeb, and Master (2013), discussed in the next chapter, refined and use the instrument to assess the extent to which school directors' use of their time across different types of tasks is correlated with student outcomes. Recent research in the United States is also using technology to improve experience sampling methods and to overcome some of the limitations with both self-reported time-use data and shadowing data (Hochbein and others 2018).

Self-reported data, as well as emerging data using more objective time-use tools, provide a glimpse of how the region's school directors spend their time. Reflecting their multifaceted responsibilities, directors in LAC self-report splitting their time across several different types of tasks, with only about 20–25 percent of time spent specifically on pedagogical activities (figure 2.9).[7] At the same time, self-reports may diverge in important ways from objective measures of directors' time use. Research on Brazil's preschools used both approaches. That research shows that 80 percent of directors' and pedagogical coordinators' actual time is taken up by instructional, operations, and safety issues, while their self-reports, as well as their ideal time allocations, are much more balanced across different types of tasks (figure 2.10). There is no clear sense of what this breakdown of time should look like, because the role of the director can vary between and within countries (depending, for example, on school size). Our limited data show that what does matter is the quality of the activities they carry out, but playing multiple roles at once with limited training and support, as school directors in many LAC countries do, may not support quality practices.

Quality of school management practices

A second set of recently developed tools measures the quality of school management practices. The World Management Survey (WMS) by Bloom and others (2015), and its adaptation for middle- and lower-income countries, the Development World Management Survey (D-WMS) by Lemos, Muralidharan, and Scur (2021), objectively measure the existence of effective practices in the areas of operations management and instructional planning, performance monitoring, target setting, human resources management, and leadership practices (table 2.1). The WMS and D-WMS are adapted from a survey methodology

FIGURE 2.9
Public school directors self-report dividing their time between many different tasks and stakeholders in Brazil, Chile, and Mexico

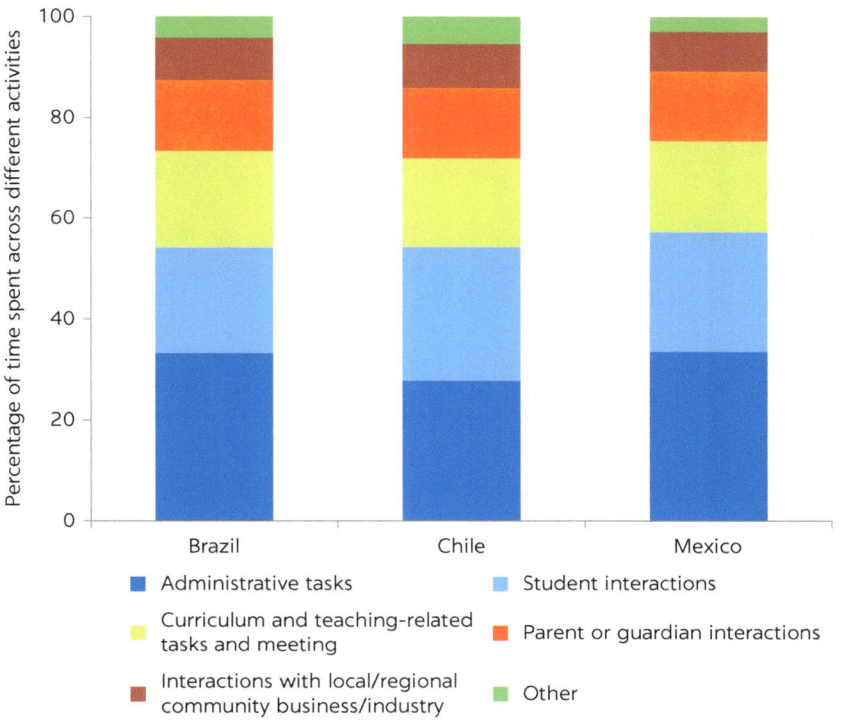

Source: World Bank.
Note: This figure shows average breakdown of time use, as reported by public secondary school directors in each country, using data from the 2013 TALIS Assessment. School weights are used to compute country-level statistics.

described in Bloom and Van Reenen (2007) and also used in the manufacturing, retail, and health care sectors. The tools focus on practices that are considered to be relevant across industries, in addition to key education-specific practices that were developed in consultation with teachers, school leaders, and sector consultants (Bloom and others 2015).

Data are collected through structured interviews with school directors by trained enumerators who score responses from 1 to 5 against a detailed scoring grid.[8,9] Double-scoring and double-blind techniques are used to guarantee the quality of interviews and consistency in scoring. By quantifying the quality of management practices, this approach enables consistent comparisons across schools and countries. Both the WMS and D-WMS are freely available instruments, but they require relatively skilled enumerators and rigorous training. Importantly, these instruments do not measure the quality of a school's director or other leaders, but rather measure only the existence and quality of the practices themselves, regardless of who specifically carries them out.[10] Bloom and others (2015) report average management scores of schools for eight countries globally: Brazil, Canada, Germany, India, Italy, Sweden, the United Kingdom, and the United States. Across these countries, the adoption of modern managerial practices in schools is limited: the average score across all countries is 2.27 (on a scale of 1 to 5), which corresponds to a low level of adoption of many

FIGURE 2.10
Substantial differences in actual, perceived, and ideal time allocation for school directors and pedagogical directors in childhood education centers in Brazil

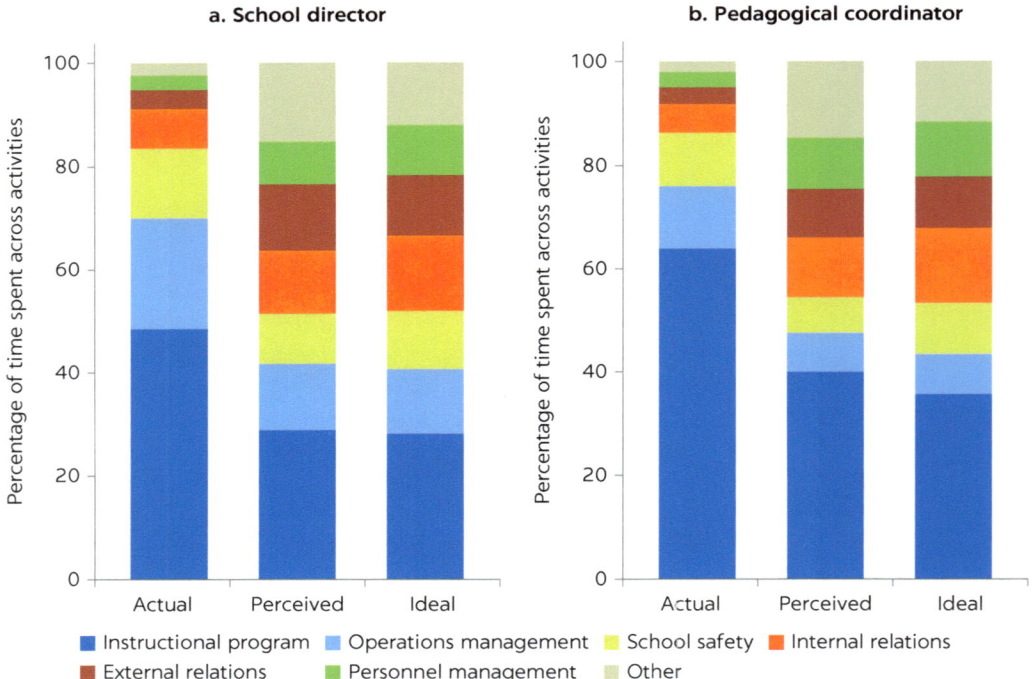

Source: World Bank calculations based on data from Almeida and others, forthcoming.
Note: This figure shows how school directors and pedagogical coordinators in early childhood education centers in Ceará, Brazil, use their time, on average, according to different methods of data collection. "Actual" refers to time use collected by reconstructing the schedule of activities over two days, via interview at the end of the second day where information about activities is recorded in increments of 15 minutes. "Perceived" refers to time use as estimated by the manager, collected via interview asking about the percentage of time spent across these different topics. "Ideal" refers to time use as ideal for the manager to effectively do the job, collected via interview asking about the percentage of time the manager would like to devote to the different topics. Number of observations: 658 (school director = 374, pedagogical coordinator = 284).

TABLE 2.1 Management practices measured in World Management Survey (WMS)

	MANAGEMENT PRACTICE	MEASURES WHETHER …
1	Standardization of instructional planning processes	School uses meaningful processes that allow pupils to learn over time.
2	Personalization of instruction and learning	School incorporates teaching methods that ensure all students can master the learning objectives.
3	Data-driven planning and transitions	School uses assessment and easily available data to verify learning outcomes at critical stages.
4	Adopting educational best practices	School incorporates and shares teaching best practices and strategies across classrooms.
5	Continuous improvement	School implements processes toward continuous improvement and encourages lessons to be captured and documented.
6	Performance tracking	School performance is regularly tracked with useful metrics.
7	Performance review	School performance is reviewed with appropriate metrics.
8	Performance dialogue	School performance is discussed with appropriate content, depth and communicated to teachers.
9	Consequence management	School has mechanisms to follow up on performance issues.

(continued)

TABLE 2.1 continued

	MANAGEMENT PRACTICE	MEASURES WHETHER …
10	Target balance	School targets cover a sufficiently broad set of goals at the school, department, and student levels.
11	Target interconnection	School established well-aligned targets across all levels.
12	Time horizon	School has a rational approach to planning and setting targets.
13	Target stretch	School sets targets with the appropriate level of difficulty.
14	Clarity and comparability of targets	School sets understandable targets and openly communicates and compares school, department, and individual performance.
15	Rewarding high performers	School implements a systematic approach to identifying good and bad performance.
16	Fixing poor performance	School deals with underperformers promptly—not necessarily firing teachers, but ensuring underperformance is acknowledged and addressed appropriately.
17	Promoting high performers	School promotes employees based on job performance rather than simply tenure.
18	Managing talent	School nurtures and develops teaching and leadership talent.
19	Retaining talent	School attempts to retain teachers with high performance.
20	Creating a distinctive employee value proposition	School has a thought-out approach to attract the best employees.

Source: Bloom and others 2015.

of the practices included in the questionnaire. Notably, country fixed effects account for 46 percent of the variance in school management scores, compared with 13 percent in manufacturing and 40 percent in hospitals across the same subset of countries and questions. This finding suggests that institutions play a particularly important role in management practices in the education sector (for example, Fuchs and Woessmann 2007).

Since Bloom and others (2015) published this work, six other countries have been added to this dataset: Colombia, Mexico, Haiti, Indonesia, Tanzania, and Pakistan. The distribution of scores in public schools shows substantial variation in the quality of management within each country surveyed across LAC and non-LAC countries (figure 2.11). Across high-income countries with higher average scores, very few surveyed schools score below 2 (for example, in the United Kingdom and Canada), whereas in countries with lower average scores, such as Brazil, Colombia, Pakistan, Mexico, and Italy, the majority of schools score below 2. A score below 2 indicates very poor management practices—almost no monitoring, very weak targets, and extremely weak incentives. At the other end of the distribution, all the surveyed middle- and high-income countries have at least some schools scoring above 3, which would correspond to medium to widespread adoption of the management practices (some reasonable performance monitoring, a mix of targets and performance-based promotion, and rewards and steps taken to address persistent underperformance). In contrast, no surveyed school in Haiti or Tanzania scores above 3.

To measure the quality of school management practices in a wider sample of countries, Leaver, Lemos, and Scur (2019) develop a new PISA-based school management index that maps the WMS questionnaire to the 2012 PISA school questionnaire. Their index captures detailed information about the level of adoption of structured management best practices in the areas of

FIGURE 2.11
Quality of school management practices in public schools varies substantially across and within countries according to the World Management Survey index

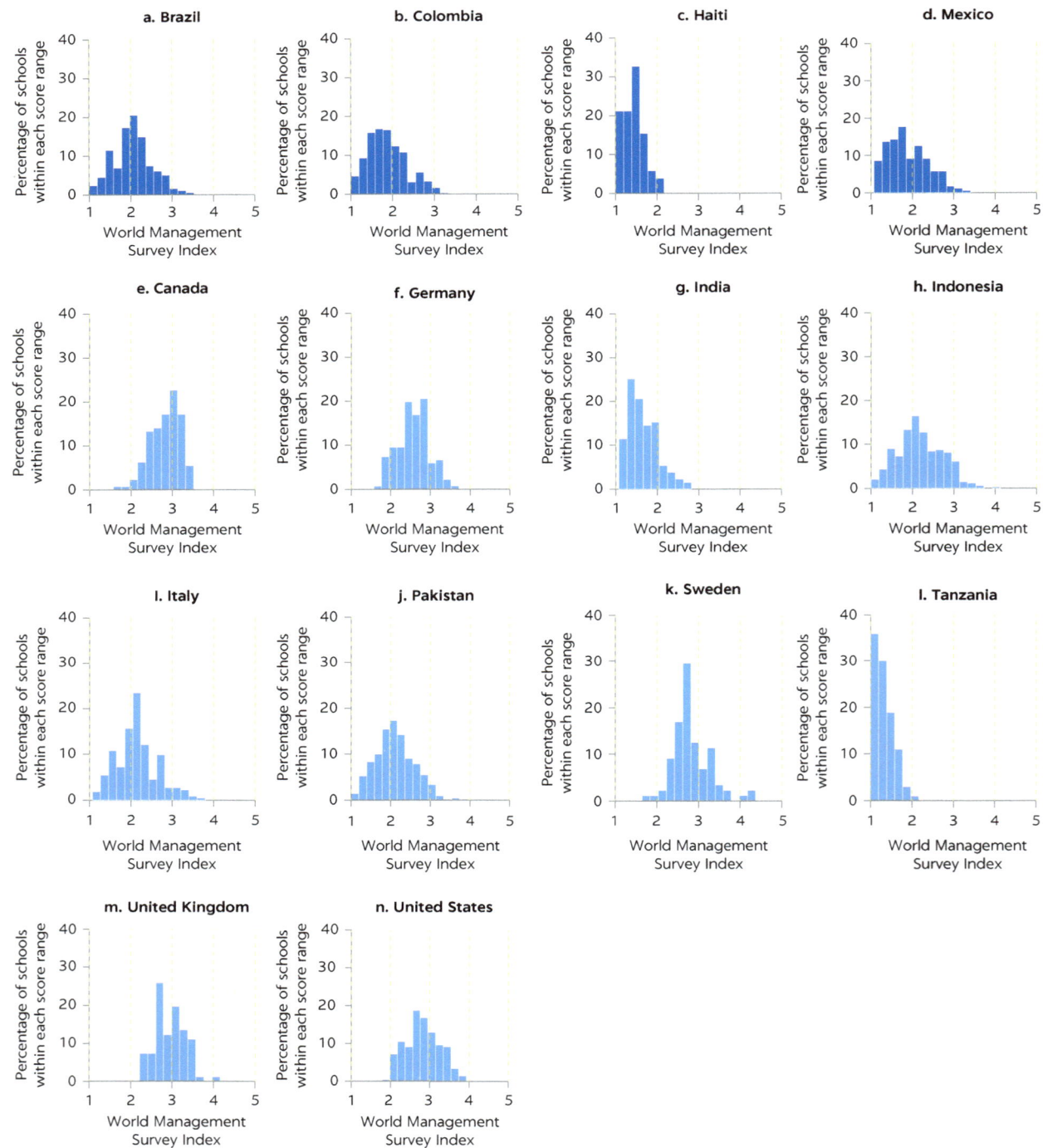

Sources: World Bank calculations based on data from Bloom and others 2015; Lemos and Scur 2016; Indonesia, Tanzania and Pakistan WB-SABER.
Note: This figure shows the distributions of school management scores collected across multiple waves of the World Management Survey and Development World Management Survey across a range of different samples in participating countries. In all countries, samples include public (government) schools and private schools receiving government support, if any. Samples for Brazil, Canada, Germany, India, Italy, Sweden, the United Kingdom, and the United States include only schools offering education to 15-year-olds. Samples for Colombia, Haiti, Indonesia, Mexico, Pakistan, and Tanzania include only primary schools and were surveyed using the Development World Management Survey. The school management score is constructed from 14 questions that are common across all samples. Number of observations: 2,564 (Brazil = 375; Colombia = 447; Haiti = 52; Mexico = 178; Canada = 128; Germany = 136; India = 131; Indonesia = 350; Italy = 222; Pakistan = 419; Sweden = 88, Tanzania = 100; United Kingdom = 81; United States = 207).

operations management (day-to-day operations, performance monitoring, and target setting) and people management in schools (Bloom and others 2015).[11] This new management index aligns well with the WMS index, indicating that meaningful information on management can be drawn from large-scale datasets like PISA.

Management of shocks in schools

Progress has also been made in measuring how schools manage shocks such as natural disasters. The School Disaster Management Survey (SDMS) developed by Adelman, Baron, and Lemos (forthcoming) aims to capture a school's current practices for dealing with potential natural disasters in the future (hurricane, flood, storm, earthquake, and landslide). The DPMS is based on a range of policy guidance and best practice literature and covers 10 topics measuring the quality of management practices in the areas of risk assessment, preparation and mitigation measures to deal with potential disaster, responses postdisaster, and distribution of disaster-related roles and responsibilities (table 2.2).[12] Given the prevalence of natural disasters in LAC and other regions, the SDMS could be used across countries to understand the quality of others' practices and learn how to further strengthen schools' resilience to natural disasters through improved management, as a complement to infrastructure programs.

TABLE 2.2 **Management practices measured in the School Disaster Management Survey (SDMS)**

	MANAGEMENT PRACTICE	MEASURES WHETHER...
1	Assessing and dealing with potential risks posed by the external environment	School has formally assessed and is able to identify potential disaster-related risks posed by the immediate school environment to staff, students, and the community and has taken steps to address and reduce these risks.
2	Assessing and dealing with potential risks posed by the school building	Quality and resilience of the school infrastructure are assessed regularly and whether reparations or improvements (if needed) are done in a proactive manner.
3	Mobilizing and training staff and students for disaster response	School has identified the types of disaster response skills needed; has frequently trained staff, teachers, and students on skills needed for disaster response; and has communicated disaster response plans to stakeholders.
4	Providing emergency supplies and shelter	School is prepared to provide emergency supplies and shelter to students and staff in case the area is affected by a natural disaster during school hours.
5	Communicating with stakeholders	School has a clear communication system for emergencies during natural disasters.
6	Taking steps to prevent damage/loss to furniture and materials	School takes clear action to prevent damage to or loss of furniture and materials, and proactively assigns this responsibility across staff members.
7	Taking steps to prevent loss of school information	School takes clear action to prevent loss of school data by regularly making copies of all basic, day-to-day and critical data, and keeping it in a safe place in order to quickly respond to a disaster and ensure educational continuity.
8	Planning use of shared resources postdisaster	School can identify local resources and assets and has a clear plan on how to share these resources with the community postdisaster.
9	Reintegrating students and teachers and resuming classes	School has a clear plan for reintegrating students and teachers and resuming classes to ensure accelerated learning and educational continuity postdisaster.
10	Distribution of clear roles and responsibilities across the school	School has defined clear roles, has distributed responsibilities for disaster preparedness across the school, and has communicated these roles and responsibilities to all relevant parties.

Source: Adelman, Baron, and Lemos, forthcoming.

Following the methodology of the D-WMS, the SDMS instrument has a scoring grid that ranges from 1 to 5, but it also allows for scores of half points to capture more variation and use of built-in techniques during its implementation to guarantee high-quality data collection. The score for each topic is obtained after triangulating the responses to several questions. These scores are used to build an average SDMS index. In Haiti, after Hurricane Matthew hit the country in 2016, the average score on this index was 1.77, meaning that, on average, schools have some informal practices in place; no school scores above a 3, and 22 percent of schools score between 2 and 3, meaning they do have some good, but informal, practices in place (figure 2.12).

Management of the system

To quantify and consistently measure elements of the organizational structure of education systems in aggregate, Adelman and others (forthcoming) have developed a new instrument, the Education System Coherence Survey (ESCS).

FIGURE 2.12

High prevalence of weak practices, yet important variation in the adoption of disaster preparedness and mitigation practices across schools in Haiti after a major hurricane according to a new School Disaster Management Survey index

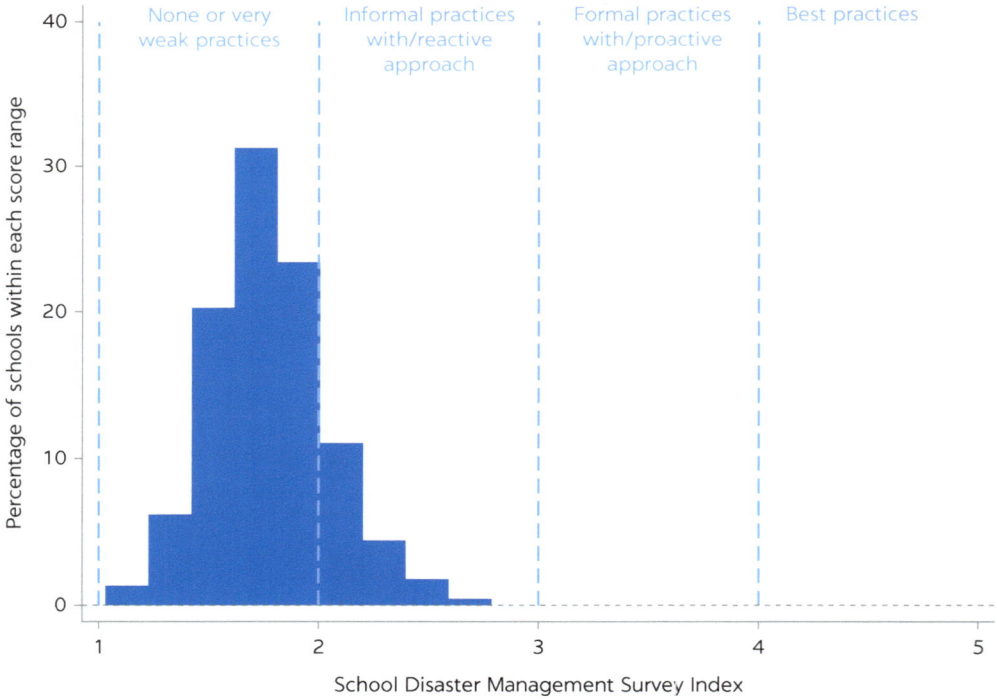

Source: World Bank calculations based on data from Adelman, Baron, and Lemos, forthcoming.
Note: This figure shows the distribution of School Disaster Management Survey scores for primary schools (public and private) collected by Adelman, Baron, and Lemos (forthcoming). The scores include survey noise controls. Mean = 1.77, SD = 0.30. Scoring follows the Development World Management Survey methodology: a score between 1 and 2 refers to a school with practically no structured practices or very weak practices implemented; a score between 2 and 3 refers to a school with some informal practices implemented, but these practices consist mostly of a reactive approach to dealing with the aftermath of disasters; a score between 3 and 4 refers to a school that has a good, formal process in place (though not yet often or consistent enough), and these practices consist mostly of a proactive approach to dealing with the aftermath of disasters; a score between 4 and 5 refers to well-defined strong practices in place that are often seen as best practices in dealing with the aftermath of disasters. Number of observations: 227.

The ESCS draws on Pritchett and Pande (2006) to identify a core set of 10 functions under the purview of most public basic education systems, and further breaks down each function into specific tasks along three dimensions—planning, implementation, and monitoring (table 2.3).

On the basis of this set of 10 functions broken down into 51 tasks, Adelman and others (forthcoming) develop three sets of data collection instruments as part of the ESCS: (a) a survey for school directors; (b) a survey for system

TABLE 2.3 Core functions of an education system measured using the Education System Coherence Survey

		TASKS IDENTIFIED ACROSS THREE DIMENSIONS OF EACH FUNCTION		
	FUNCTION	**MONITORING/IDENTIFICATION**	**PLANNING**	**IMPLEMENTATION**
1	Curriculum design	Identifying gaps or issues in the current mandatory curriculum	Deciding to make changes to the mandatory curriculum	Training teachers on the use of new materials, pedagogical methods, directives, and so on, if the curriculum were to be updated
2	Infrastructure planning	Identifying and communicating needs for school physical expansion	Deciding to initiate the physical expansion	Managing the construction or expansion process
3	Quality improvement	Establishing standards for school quality	Deciding what school quality improvements should be implemented	Assessing progress in school quality improvement
4	School selection	Evaluating the appropriateness of current student admission rules and mechanisms	Determining student admission rules and mechanisms	Carrying out the student admission process
5	Teacher hiring	Identifying and communicating needs for new teachers	Setting qualification requirements and selection processes	Carrying out selection processes, making hiring decisions, and making assignment decisions
6	Teacher supervision	Assessing the quality of in-service teachers' work	Establishing a framework for in-service teacher training, teacher compensation rules and changes, and teacher reassignment rules	Overseeing the implementation of in-service teacher training (implementation); deciding on consequences based on the quality of teachers' work, such as salary adjustments, training, firing, or relocation
7	Director hiring	Assessing and communicating needs for new directors	Establishing qualification requirements for school directors	Implementing the selection process, making hiring decisions, and making assignment decisions
8	Director supervision	Assessing the quality of directors' work	Establishing a framework for pre- and in-service director training and compensation rules and changes, and director reassignment rules	Overseeing the implementation of pre- and in-service director training; deciding on consequences based on the quality of directors' work, such as salary adjustments, training, firing, or reallocation
9	Student learning assessments	Analyzing the evaluation results and identifying progress, strengths, and weaknesses in student learning	Developing standardized student learning evaluations	Carrying out and overseeing the standardized student learning evaluation; disseminating the evaluation results to the public
10	Materials procurement	Identifying and communicating the needs for school materials such as books or furniture; overseeing an independent review of whether funds for acquisition of materials were spent appropriately	Approving a budget for purchasing needed school materials	Making large and small purchases of school materials

Source: Adelman and others, forthcoming.

authorities at the national, subnational, and local levels; and (c) a legislative review. The ESCS was successfully applied in public basic education systems of four LAC countries—Brazil, the Dominican Republic, Guatemala, and Peru—with different system structures. The data are used to construct several new measures of the completeness, coherence, and quality of the functioning of public basic education systems. The initial sample for each country was selected randomly from among public schools located in the local-level administrative units (for example, municipalities) where system officials were also interviewed. The school director survey was carried out by a survey firm via phone calls to a sample of 50–100 directors per country. Structured interviews with system authorities were carried out by a local education sector senior expert in each country, using an instrument that asks about task allocation as well as asks follow-up questions to gauge whether the tasks claimed by a government official as belonging to his or her level of the system are actually carried out, and with what results. The legislative review describes the de jure allocation of tasks in the education system as defined by current regulation. The review, which was performed by the same local education sector expert in each country, identifies which level of the system (national, subnational, local, or school) is allocated specific tasks.

FIGURE 2.13

Substantial variation in the incoherence of task allocation across and within countries according to a new Education System Coherence Survey

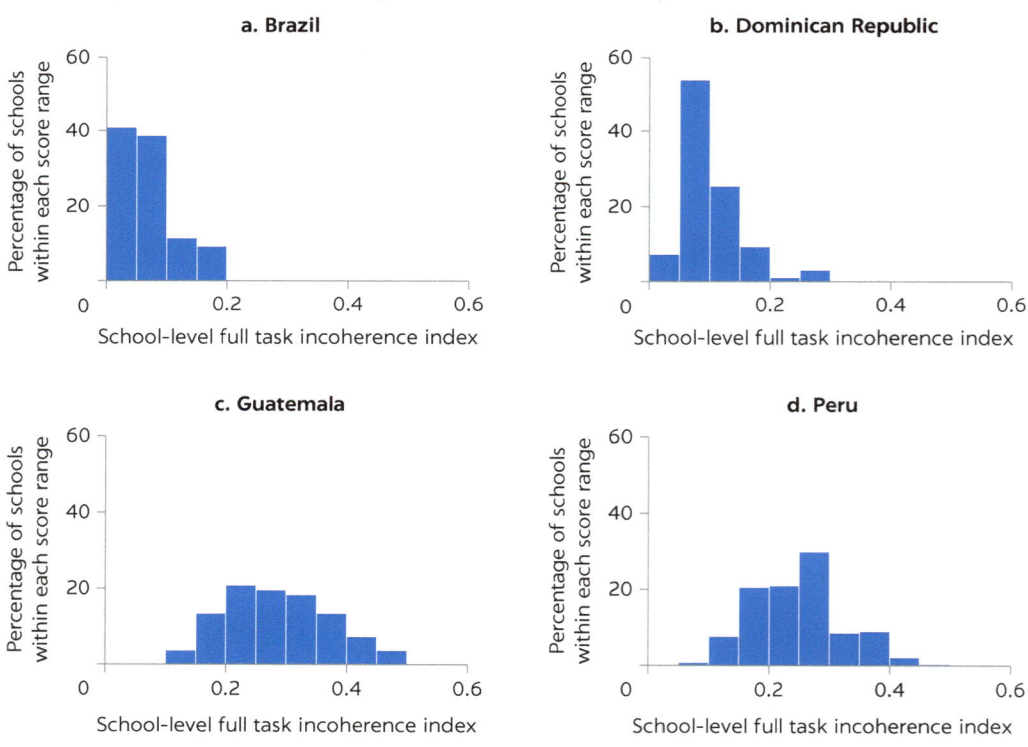

Source: World Bank calculations based on data from Adelman and others, forthcoming.
Note: This figure shows the distribution of the school-level full incoherence index—that is, the average percentage of incoherent tasks for schools in Brazil, the Dominican Republic, Guatemala, and Peru. Full incoherence takes the value of 1 if the local official, school director, and legislation do not allocate the task to the same education system level and 0 if they do agree fully or partially. The percentage of incoherent tasks by school is the number of fully incoherent tasks as a percentage of the total tasks. Number of school-level observations per country: Brazil = 44, Dominican Republic = 98, Guatemala = 82, and Peru = 100.

One of the several measures that can be constructed from this survey is a measure of incoherence between the de jure allocation, the local bureaucrat's and school director's de facto understanding of the allocation, and execution of the tasks that make up the core functions of an education system. For each one of the 51 tasks identified, full incoherence takes the value of 1 if bureaucrats, school principals, and legislation do not allocate the task to the same level in the education system, and 0 if they agree fully or partially. The full incoherence index at the school level reflects the number of fully incoherent tasks as a percentage of total tasks. Although the results of this and other measures are detailed in the next chapter, a distribution of the index reveals existing variation within and across all four countries, highlighting the value of instruments designed to collect more granular data for better measurement (figure 2.13).

Each of these instruments represents important progress in generating comparable data on management in education. It is important to note that these instruments have several shortcomings, including the focus on a limited set of practices and system attributes. Yet, collecting data on many dimensions of management at the same time puts a heavy burden on respondents. Together, however, this set of measurement tools provides policy makers, practitioners, and researchers with useful resources for creating snapshots of how well developed management practices are in a school or at other levels of an education system. The results allow them to identify specific areas where practices can be strengthened, to track the impacts of policy changes or programs on practices, and possibly to provide feedback to individual managers about opportunities to improve their own performance.[13]

NOTES

1. One challenge that likely limits the use of these questionnaires from international student assessments is that the questions are seldom consistent over different rounds of the same assessment or across different assessments, limiting longitudinal comparisons and the number of countries that can be compared on the same measure.
2. Evidence of the effects of different selection methods on the quality of the individuals selected is discussed in chapter 4.
3. Given the evidence that autonomy in and of itself is not a good or bad policy, these results are presented as descriptive facts that can inform the design of approaches to strengthen management and not as evaluative statements.
4. Also, 77 percent of the programs surveyed are offered to school directors in basic education, among other levels of education.
5. Breaking down by management topic, one dimension that seems to be less emphasized in training program content is people management. In LAC, given the lack of autonomy of many schools in the public sector to recruit or dismiss their own teachers, it is not a surprising omission. However, this might be a missed opportunity because there are people management practices that can be adopted by school directors, despite the lack of autonomy, to reward and promote well-performing teachers in different ways.
6. The share of programs providing in-school support is much lower both during and after training. In fact, 54 percent of programs provide in-school support from trainers and facilitators during the training, while this number falls to 23 percent when the training has ended. In-school support from others such as other school directors and school staff is much lower: 31 percent and 15 percent, respectively, during the training, and 8 percent and 0 percent, respectively, after the training has ended.
7. Self-reported time allocation does vary depending on the option set provided to respondents. For example, in the 2006 SERCE (Second Regional Comparative and Explanatory Study) assessment in Latin America, directors reported spending about 30–35 percent of their time on pedagogical activities.

8. Scores are in whole points for the WMS and half points for the D-WMS to capture more variation in the left tail of the distribution.
9. A score of 1 means worst practice or no practice in place, a score of 2 means the school has something in place, but its practices are reactive, a score of 3 means the school has a good process in place, but with some weaknesses, a score of 4 means the school has a good process in place, and its practices are proactive, and a score of 5 means best practice in management.
10. As discussed in chapter 3, the WMS has also been adapted to measure management practices within defined units of a public bureaucracy.
11. The Leaver, Lemos, and Scur (2019) paper is described in detail in chapter 3. As previously discussed, the ability to construct such indexes using international data such as PISA hinges on the consistency of questionnaires over time. In the case of PISA, the subsequent rounds (2015 and 2018) did not include the same extent of questions as 2012 and therefore were not used by Leaver, Lemos, and Scur (2019).
12. These works include a manual for preparing for and responding to emergencies for UNICEF education program officers (UNICEF ROSA 2006); guides for disaster prevention in schools, for education sector decision-makers (Petal 2008); guides for crisis planning, school emergency, and disaster preparedness for schools and communities (Oreta 2010; US Department of Education 2007); guides for disaster risk reduction (DRR) for teachers (UNESCO 2014); guides for emergency management at institutions of higher education (US Department of Education 2010); compilation of good practices and lessons learned for DRR at schools (UNISDR and UNESCO 2007), among others. The tool was prepared in consultation with World Bank specialists in disaster risk management.
13. Appendix table A1 provides a detailed comparison across three of the instruments described in this chapter that measure management practices at the school level, along with measures included in recent large international student assessments.

REFERENCES

Adelman, Melissa, Renata Lemos, Reema Nayar, and Maria Jose Vargas. Forthcoming. "(In)coherence in the Management of Education Systems in Latin America." Working paper. World Bank, Washington, DC.

Adelman, Melissa, Juan Baron, and Renata Lemos. Forthcoming. "Managing Shocks in Education: Evidence from Hurricane Matthew in Haiti." Working paper. World Bank, Washington, DC.

Almeida, Rita, Leandro Costa, Ildo Lautharte, and Renata Lemos. Forthcoming. "Managerial Time Allocation and Student Learning: Evidence from Brazil." Working paper. World Bank, Washington, DC.

Barrera-Osorio, Felipe, Tazeen Fasih, Harry Anthony Patrinos, and Lucrecia Santibañez. 2009. *Decentralized Decision-Making in Schools. The Theory and Evidence on School-Based Management.* Directions in Development Series. Washington, DC: World Bank.

Blimpo, Moussa Pouguinimpo, David Evans, and Nathalie Lahire. 2015. "Parental Human Capital and Effective School Management. Evidence from The Gambia." Policy Research Working Paper 7238, World Bank, Washington, DC.

Bloom, Nicholas, Renata Lemos, Raffaella Sadun, and John Van Reenen. 2015. "Does Management Matter in Schools?" *The Economic Journal* 125 (584): 647–74.

Bloom, Nicholas, and John Van Reenen. 2007. "Measuring and Explaining Management Practices across Firms and Countries." *Quarterly Journal of Economics*, 122(4): 1351–1408.

Borman, Geoffrey, Gina Hewes, Laura Overman, and Shelly Brown. 2003. "Comprehensive School Reform and Achievement: A Meta-Analysis." *Review of Educational Research* 73 (2): 125–230.

Bruns, Barbara, Deon Filmer, and Harry Patrinos. 2011. *Making Schools Work. New Evidence on Accountability Reforms.* Human Development Perspectives. Washington, DC: World Bank.

Bush, Tony. 2019. "Distinguishing Between Educational Leadership and Management: Compatible or Incompatible Constructs?" *Educational Management Administration & Leadership.*

Carr-Hill, Roy. 2017. "Accountability in Education: Meeting our Commitments. Exploring the Composition of School Councils and its Relationship to Council Effectiveness as an Accountability Tool." Background paper commissioned for the 2017/2018 Global Education Monitoring Report.

Connolly, Michael, Chris James, and Michael Fertig. 2019. "The Difference between Educational Management and Educational Leadership and the Importance of Educational Responsibility." *Educational Management Administration & Leadership* 47 (4): 504–19.

Di Gropello, Emanuela. 2006. *A Comparative Analysis of School-Based Management in Central America*. World Bank Working Paper No. 72. Washington, DC: World Bank.

Flessa, Joseph, Daniela Bramwell, Magdalena Fernandez, and José Weinstein. 2018. "School Leadership in Latin America 2000–2016." *Educational Management Administration & Leadership* 46 (2): 182–206.

Fuchs, Thomas, and Ludger Woessmann. 2007. "What Accounts for International Differences in Student Performance? A Re-examination Using PISA Data." *Empirical Economics* 32 (2): 433–64.

Gipson, Asha, Danielle Pfaff, David Mendelsohn, Lauren Catenacci, and W. Warner Burke. 2017. "Women and Leadership: Selection, Development, Leadership Style, and Performance." *Journal of Applied Behavioral Science* 53 (1): 32–65.

Grissom, Jason, Susanna Loeb, and Benjamin Master. 2013. "Effective Instructional Time Use for School Leaders: Longitudinal Evidence from Observations of Principals." *Educational Researcher* 42 (8): 433–44.

Hochbein, Craig, Bridget V. Dever, George White, Linda Mayger, and Emily Gallagher. 2018. "Confronting Methodological Challenges in Studying School Leader Time Use through Technological Advancements: A Pilot Study." *Educational Management Administration & Leadership* 46 (4): 659–78.

Horng, Eileen, Daniel Klasik, and Susanna Loeb. 2010. "Principal Time-Use and School Effectiveness." *American Journal of Education* 116 (4): 491–523.

Leaver, Clare, Renata Lemos, and Daniela Scur. 2019. "Measuring and Explaining Management in Schools: New Approaches Using Public Data." Policy Research Working Paper 9053, World Bank, Washington, DC.

Lemos, Renata, Karthik Muralidharan, and Daniela Scur. 2021. "Personnel Management and School Productivity: Evidence from India." NBER Working Paper 28336, National Bureau of Economic Research, Cambridge, MA.

Lemos, Renata, and Daniela Scur. 2016. "Developing Management: An Expanded Evaluation Tool for Developing Countries." RISE Working Paper 16/007. Oxford: Research on Improving Systems of Education (RISE).

López-Calva, Luis F., and Luis D. Espinosa. 2006. "Efectos diferenciales de los programas compensatorios del CONAFE en el aprovechamiento escolar." In *Efectos del Impulso a la Participación de los Padres de Familia en la Escuela*, edited by CONAFE. Mexico: CONAFE.

Martínez, Miryam, Manuel Molina-López, and Ruth Mateos de Cabo. 2020. "Explaining the Gender Gap in School Principalship: A Tale of Two Sides." *Education Management Administration & Leadership* 33: 1–20.

Nannyonjo, Harriet. 2017. "Building Capacity of School Leaders: Strategies that Work—Jamaica's Experience." World Bank.

Oreta, Andres Winston C. 2010. "Guidance Notes. School Emergency and Disaster Preparedness." Geneva: UNISDR (International Strategy for Disaster Reduction) Asia and the Pacific.

Paes de Barros, Ricardo, and Rosane Mendonça. 1998. "The Impact of Three Institutional Innovations in Brazilian Education." In *Organization Matters: Agency Problems in Health and Education in Latin America*, edited by William D. Savedoff. Washington, DC: Inter-American Development Bank.

Petal, Marla. 2008. "Disaster Prevention for Schools: Guidance for Education Sector Decision-Makers." Geneva: UNISDR (International Strategy for Disaster Reduction).

Pont, Beatriz, Deborah Nusche, and Hunter Moorman. 2008. *Improving School Leadership. Volume 1: Policy and Practice*. Paris: Organisation for Economic Co-operation and Development.

Popova, Anna, David Evans, Mary Breeding, and Violeta Arancibia. 2018. "Teacher Professional Development Around the World: The Gap Between Evidence and Practice." Policy Research Working Paper 8572, World Bank, Washington, DC.

Pradhan, Menno, Daniel Suryadarma, Amanda Beatty, Maisy Wong, Armida Alishjahbana, Arya Gaduh, and Rima Prama Artha. 2014. "Improving Educational Quality through Enhancing Community Participation: Results from a Randomized Field Experiment in Indonesia." *American Economic Journal: Applied Economics* 6 (2): 105–26.

Pritchett, Lant, and Varad Pande. 2006. "Making Primary Education Work for India's Rural Poor: A Proposal for Effective Decentralization." Social Development—South Asia Series Paper No. 95, World Bank, Washington, DC.

Santibañez, Lucrecia, Raul Abreu-Lastra, and Jennifer O'Donoghue. 2014. "School Based Management Effects: Resources or Governance Change? Evidence from Mexico." *Economics of Education Review* 39: 97–109.

Spillane, James, and Bijou Hunt. 2010. "Days of their Lives: A Mixed-Methods, Descriptive Analysis of the Men and Women at Work in the Principal's Office." *Journal of Curriculum Studies* 42 (3): 293–331.

UNESCO (United Nations Educational, Scientific and Cultural Organization). 2014. "A Teacher's Guide to Disaster Risk Reduction. Stay Safe and Be Prepared." Paris: UNESCO and UNESCO-associated schools.

UNICEF ROSA (United Nations Children's Fund Regional Office for South Asia). 2006. *Education in Emergencies. A Resource Tool Kit*. Kathmandu, Nepal: Regional Office for South Asia in Conjunction with New York Headquarters.

UNISDR (United Nations International Strategy for Disaster Reduction) and UNESCO (UN Educational, Scientific and Cultural Organization). 2007. *Towards a Culture of Prevention: Disaster Risk Reduction Begins at School—Good Practices and Lessons Learned*. Geneva: UNISDR. https://www.unisdr.org/files/761_education-good-practices.pdf.

US Department of Education, Office of Safe and Drug-Free Schools. 2007. *Practical Information on Crisis Planning. A Guide for Schools and Communities*. Washington, DC: US Department of Education.

US Department of Education, Office of Safe and Drug-Free Schools. 2010. *Action Guide for Emergency Management at Institutions of Higher Education*. Washington, DC: US Department of Education.

Weinstein, José, Ariel Azar, and Joseph Flessa. 2018. "An Ineffective Preparation? The Scarce Effect in Primary School Principals' Practices of School Leadership Preparation and Training in Seven Countries in Latin America." *Educational Management Administration & Leadership* 46 (2): 226–57.

Weinstein, José, and Macarena Hernández. 2016. "Birth Pains: Emerging School Leadership Policies in Eight School Systems of Latin America." *International Journal of Leadership in Education: Theory and Practice*. 19 (3): 241–63.

World Bank. 2007. *What Is School-Based Management?* Washington, DC: World Bank.

World Bank. 2018. *World Development Report 2018: Learning to Realize Education's Promise*. Washington, DC: World Bank.

3 How Management Matters for Education Outcomes
NEW THEORY AND EVIDENCE FROM LAC

Evidence of a strong correlation between different measures of management practices and education outcomes within countries is increasing. For example, Bloom and others (2015) show that their school management score as measured through the World Management Survey is strongly, positively correlated with school-level student outcomes across six high- and middle-income countries.[1] Using their pooled cross-country data to plot school-level student learning outcomes by each quartile of school management score reveals a strong positive correlation. For these countries, moving from the bottom to the top quartile of management is associated with a large increase in student learning outcomes, equivalent to approximately 0.4 standard deviations (figure 3.1, panel a). Leaver, Lemos, and Scur (2019) also show a similar relationship with their PISA-based management index for 2012 using data for all 65 participating countries: schools in the bottom quartile of management within their country score are, on average, about 6 points *lower* than the PISA global mean across math, reading, and science, and students in schools in the top quartile of management within their country score are, on average, about 5.5 points *higher* than the PISA global mean (figure 3.1, panel b). The authors find an even stronger positive relationship using the Prova Brasil–based management index covering nearly all public schools in Brazil: moving from the bottom to the top quartile is associated with an increase in math and reading (Portuguese) of 0.74 and 0.8 standard deviations, respectively (figure 3.1, panel c).

But how does management matter in education? This chapter presents new conceptual frameworks and empirical evidence that identifies specific channels through which management can influence education service delivery and ultimately student outcomes. The first section describes a conceptual model of the management of day-to-day activities in schools and draws on data from PISA-participating LAC countries to show how management can affect student outcomes through teachers, students, and families. The second section presents new empirical evidence on how management of shocks in schools can affect service provision and student outcomes, drawing from the experience of Hurricane Matthew in Haiti. The third section turns to the middle layers of education systems, reviewing the limited but promising research on managers and practices above the school level. The final section focuses on the system level, presenting

FIGURE 3.1

Increasing evidence of a strong positive correlation between school management practices and education outcomes in public and private schools across multiple measures and countries

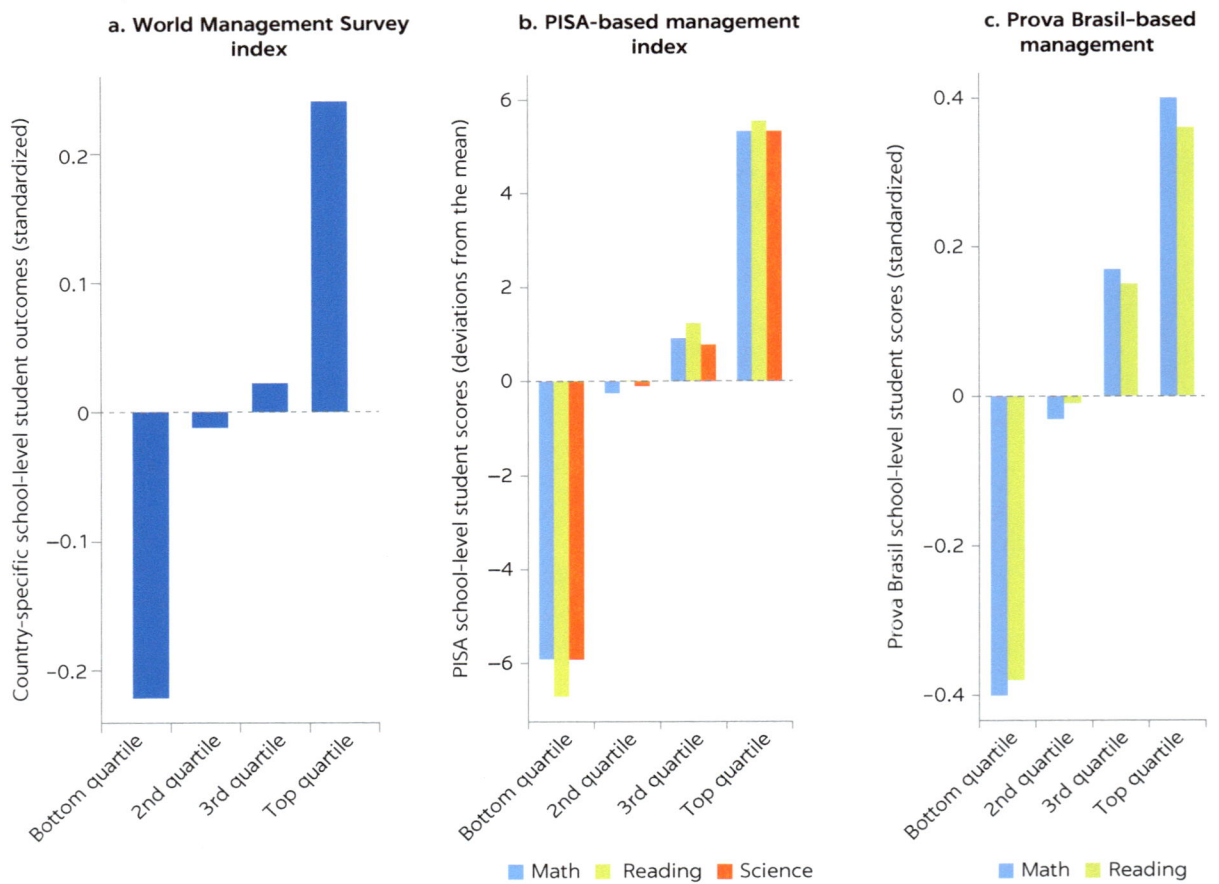

Sources: World Bank calculations based on data from Bloom and others 2015; Leaver, Lemos, and Scur 2019.
Note: This figure depicts the school management and performance at the student or school level by quartiles of the management score distribution within countries (where the bottom quartile includes the lowest 25 percent of scores, the second quartile includes up to the median score, the 3rd quartile considers from the median up to 75th percentile, and the top quartile includes the highest 25 percent of scores of each country). Panel a uses data from the World Management Survey across six countries from Bloom and others (2015), reproduced in figure B3 by Leaver, Lemos, and Scur (2019). (Number of observations = 1,002 schools.) Panel b uses data from the 2012 PISA across 65 countries from figure 2 in Leaver, Lemos, and Scur (2019). Student outcomes are estimated using five plausible values and collapsed at the school level using PISA's senate weights; test scores are presented as deviations from the global mean. (Number of observations = 15,196 schools.) Panel c uses data from the 2013 Prova Brasil in Brazil from figure 4 in Leaver, Lemos, and Scur (2019). Student learning outcomes data comes from national tests in Portuguese and math at grade 9. (Number of observations = 33,148 schools.) The management index for panel a is detailed in Bloom and others (2015); for panels b and c, it is detailed in detailed in Leaver, Lemos, and Scur (2019).

new measures and correlational evidence from Brazil, the Dominican Republic, Guatemala, and Peru on how system-level management matters for student outcomes. Taken together, these results represent important contributions to our understanding of how management matters in education, but much remains to be learned—a topic we return to in the concluding chapter.

DAY-TO-DAY SCHOOL MANAGEMENT

Better school management practices on a day-to-day basis can help ensure the availability and quality of key inputs, as well as the conditions that enable these inputs to come together and produce learning. Yet we have lacked a systematic description of the specific channels through which school management can affect student outcomes. Leaver, Lemos, and Scur (2019) begin addressing this gap by developing a simple framework that focuses specifically on the role of management in shaping the most important inputs for education—teachers, students, and families. The context of this framework is a two-sector economy: an education sector, with a set of public schools (that is, government run) and private schools (nongovernment run), and another outside sector. The dynamics of the public and private education subsectors, and the type of private sector (outside) offerings, are vastly different across countries and regions. In many countries, high-cost private schools cater to the affluent part of the population, and in a growing number of countries, there also exist low-cost private schools catering to students in the lower end of the income distribution. In the former context, private sector teaching jobs are preferred to public sector jobs and usually provide performance-based compensation schemes. In the latter, however, public sector teaching jobs are highly paid relative to the private sector. The model intends to capture the essential features of education systems in Latin America, where high-cost private schools are a substantial share of the market, and public sector teaching jobs do not confer significant rents relative to the private sector.

The framework by Leaver, Lemos, and Scur (2019) posits that management practices can affect both the behavior of teachers and households (students and their families) through selection and incentive mechanisms. Specifically, the model proposes that stronger school management practices can affect student learning outcomes because school actors such as teachers, students, and parents become more productive (incentive channel), and new actors join the school (selection channel).[2] The framework also decomposes the impact of management practices between management of operations and of people. People management practices are those intended to attract, develop, and reward teachers; those practices in turn determine the *structure* of teacher compensation (including nonpecuniary benefits). Operations management practices, on the other hand, are those in place to ensure that the quality of instruction and learning is based on data-driven decisions and is a well-monitored process with clear and achievable goals. These practices determine the *total level* of teacher compensation.[3]

Decomposing the impact between management of people and of operations is important, considering the personnel policy restrictions the public sector faces in countries in the region. In fact, the cumulative distribution functions of the Leaver, Lemos, and Scur's (2019) PISA-based people management index by public and private sectors show that across the entire range of the index, public schools fare worse than private schools. For any given lower score of people management, there is a higher share of public schools with that score relative to private schools, and for any given higher score, there is a higher share of private schools with that score relative to public schools (figure 3.2).[4]

Thus, the framework predicts that good people management practices improve student learning through two channels. A teacher exerts more effort because these practices provide extrinsic incentives and cultivate intrinsic incentives. Compounding this effect, good people management practices improve selection: a teacher with high ability and high intrinsic motivation may prefer a school with performance pay over alternative employment because she anticipates that she will work hard and be rewarded for

FIGURE 3.2
Lower quality people management practices in public schools than private schools on average across Latin America and the Caribbean

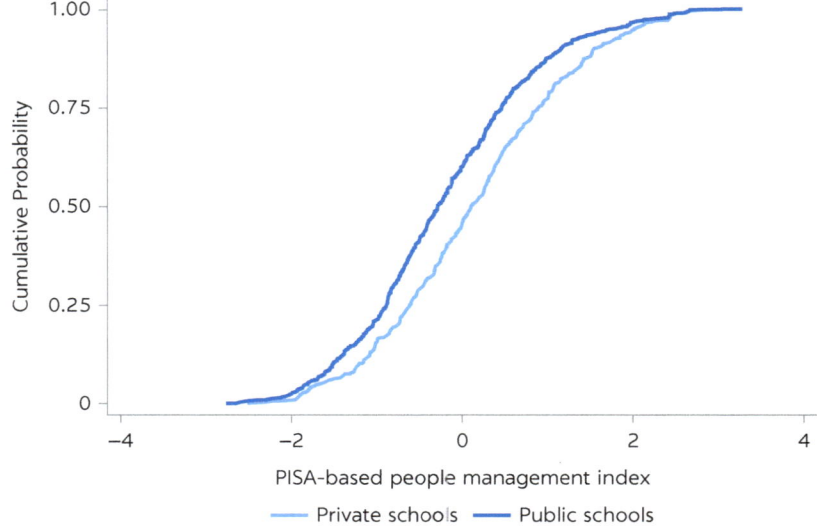

Source: Leaver, Lemos, and Scur 2019.
Note: This figure shows the cumulative distribution of the PISA-based people management index for private and public schools for eight Latin American countries participating in PISA in 2012. The people management index is built out of the school questionnaire from PISA 2012 and is detailed in Leaver, Lemos, and Scur (2019). Number of observations: 3,069 (2,432 public schools, 637 private schools).

producing student learning. The framework also predicts that good operations management practices improve student learning through two channels. There is no teacher incentive effect but the selection effect remains, now driven by the *level* rather than the *structure* of compensation. This is reinforced by a household incentive effect that arises because strong operations management practices encourage both students and parents to increase their inputs.

The authors support these predictions using PISA data from LAC countries. First, directors in schools with higher PISA-based people management scores (predominantly private schools) are less likely to report experiencing teacher shortages and are also more likely to report higher levels of teacher motivation and effort, compared with directors in schools with lower PISA-based people management scores (figure 3.3, panel a). Second, directors in public schools with higher PISA-based operations management scores are less likely to report experiencing teacher shortages and also more likely to report higher levels of teacher motivation, teacher effort, and household effort, compared with directors in public schools with lower PISA-based operations management scores (figure 3.3, panel b).

These results help shed light on the findings of several strands of related literature that examine the relationship between management practices, teachers, and student outcomes. First, several studies that use rich administrative and survey data from various districts in the United States suggest that across public schools, those that attract and retain better teachers, improve those teachers' skills more quickly, and cultivate safe and collaborative school climates for

FIGURE 3.3
Both people and operations management play a role in improving learning through selection and incentive channels

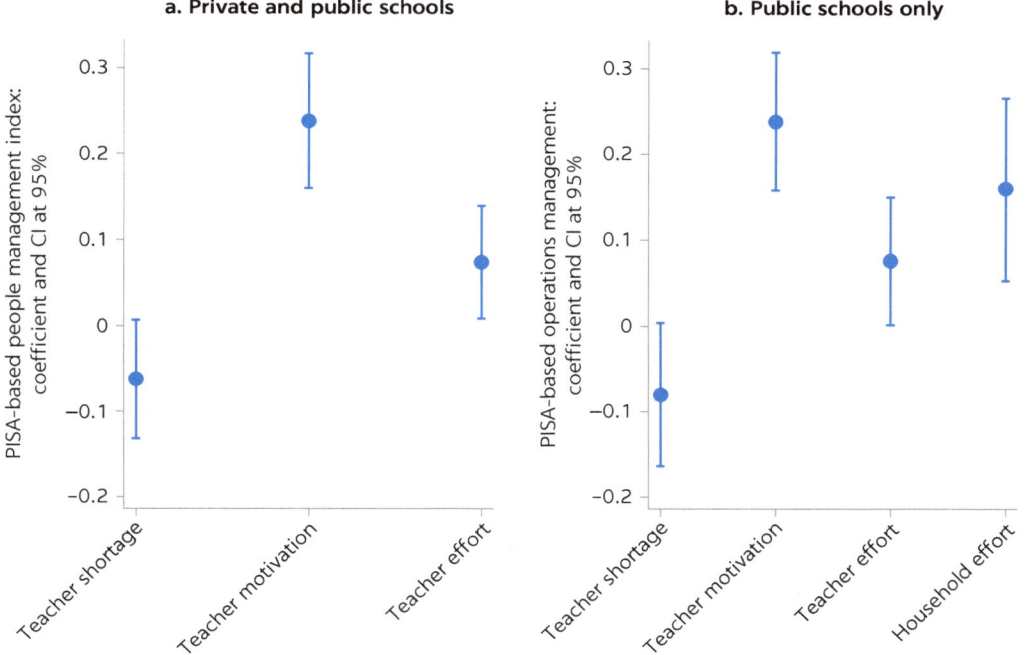

Source: Leaver, Lemos, and Scur 2019, tables 3 and 4.
Note: This figure covers eight Latin American countries participating in PISA. In panel a, it plots the coefficient and 95 percent confidence intervals (CIs) of separate regressions of the PISA-based people management index on three teacher indexes—shortage, motivation, and effort—for private and public schools (table 3). Panel b plots the coefficient and 95 percent confidence intervals of separate regressions of the PISA-based operations management index for the same three teacher indexes and a household effort index (table 4). All indexes are also built from the 2012 PISA school questionnaire and are detailed in Leaver, Lemos, Scur (2019). Number of observations: 3,069 (2,432 public schools, 637 private schools).

teachers and students—all indicators of stronger people and operations management practices—are those with higher student achievement (for example, Grissom and Loeb 2011; Kraft, Marinell, and Yee 2016; Sebastian and Allensworth 2012) or value added (a measure of how much students learn in school; see Branch, Hanushek, and Rivkin 2012; Grissom and Bartanen 2019; Loeb, Kalogrides, and Béteille 2012). Studies of teachers' perceptions also show that teachers who assess their school management as more effective and supportive have higher job satisfaction and are less likely to plan to leave their job (Ladd 2011; Stockard and Lehman 2004).

Other research has begun examining detailed people and operations management practices in observational and experimental settings to better understand their individual impacts, primarily in the United States. Using detailed time-use data from direct observation of school directors in Miami-Dade County Florida, Grissom, Loeb, and Master (2013) show that directors' time spent on structured instruction activities, such as developing the school's educational program or conducting planned classroom observations, is positively correlated with growth in student achievement, while time spent on unstructured activities such as informal classroom walkthroughs is negatively correlated. A small number of randomized trials are beginning to show that improvements in specific people and operations management practices that are feasible within public schools, where there is little scope for variation in the pecuniary elements of teacher compensation, can actually have important impacts. For example, structured and detailed feedback on classroom practices and structured, data-based peer-to-peer learning activities have both been shown to significantly improve teaching practices and subsequent student learning in different US school districts, even though they were tied to relatively low-powered incentives (Papay and others 2020; Taylor and Tyler 2012).

Finally, a third strand of research has highlighted how people management practices can depend in complex ways on school directors' or others' incentives. For example, Grissom, Kalogrides, and Loeb (2017) show that primary school directors in Florida engage in strategic staffing by reassigning their most effective teachers to grades with high-stakes standardized exams to raise scores in the short term, with the unintended consequence of concentrating less effective teachers in early grades and lowering student achievement in the long term. In China, Li (2018) uses novel data to show that secondary school directors, who have substantial influence over teacher promotion decisions, favor their close social connections and that this bias reduces the effort of unfavored teachers and induces the most effective ones to leave. In Ghana, Beg, Fitzpatrick, and Lucas (2021) measure whether there is gender bias in principals' assessment of teacher effectiveness by collecting data from principals' subjective evaluations and teachers' self-evaluations and objective effectiveness. The authors find that principals are 11 percentage points less likely to rate a female teacher as "more effective," despite female teachers being objectively more effective based on student learning than male teachers.

This theory and supporting empirical evidence therefore begin to get inside the black box of how day-to-day school management affects student outcomes. Yet many questions remain for future research, including how management affects families' decisions about which school to select for their student (a topic we return to in the concluding chapter).

MANAGING SHOCKS IN SCHOOLS

In addition to affecting the day-to-day work of schools, better management practices can help schools deal with shocks of various types, including influxes of new students, major budget cuts, natural disasters, and public health crises. Shocks have been shown to affect student achievement in both basic and tertiary education, with a large body of literature drawing primarily from high- and upper-middle-income countries. For example, regarding influxes of students see Gould, Lavy, and Paserman (2009). For budget shocks see Chakrabarti, Livingston, and Setren (2015); Deming and Walters (2017); and Jackson, Wigger, and Xiong (2018). For natural disasters, see DiPietro (2018). For public health crises, see Bandiera and others (2020) and Archibong and Annan (2020). This research generally does not delve into *how* schools react to these shocks, yet management practices are potentially an important channel through which school leaders could mitigate the impacts. For example, better monitoring practices can help identify areas of need and enable the rapid reallocation of budget or human resources in response to changing conditions, such as an influx of new students. Better management of operations and people can help in creating and following emergency response plans and having support from a cohesive network of stakeholders after a natural disaster.

Natural disasters are an especially relevant type of shock for this study, as the LAC region has the highest per capita rate of natural disasters globally, with hurricanes in particular expected to continue increasing in number and strength (Gutmann and others 2018; NOAA 2018; World Bank 2018). The importance of reestablishing education as soon as possible after a natural disaster is widely shared among experts and advocated in the humanitarian literature (UNESCO 2014; US Department of Education 2007; UNICEF ROSA 2006); however, the direct impact of school management on the speed and degree of recovery from disasters has not previously been studied empirically.[5]

Adelman, Baron, and Lemos (forthcoming) provide evidence of the role of management practices in mitigating the impact of a natural disaster, with data from Haiti before and after Hurricane Matthew, which made landfall as a Category 4 storm in October 2016. Haiti's low level of development and its geography make it vulnerable to a range of natural disasters, including the earthquake that caused catastrophic damage and loss of life in the capital Port-au-Prince and surrounding areas in 2010 (World Bank 2013). In addition, over 80 percent of primary schools are private, owned and operated by a constellation of religious groups, nonprofit organizations, and private citizens (Adelman, Holland, and Heidelk 2017). In this context, most schools receive limited or no support from either national or local governments in the aftermath of shocks, including Hurricane Matthew. Therefore it is largely up to individual schools or school networks to obtain support and recover, creating a context in which school management practices could play an important role in determining the effects of shocks.

The policy literature on education and disasters identifies several channels through which management may help determine how schools are affected by and recover from natural disasters. First, the day-to-day management practices of a school can affect how well-prepared it is to face a disaster. Regular maintenance of infrastructure and well-organized document management are considered good practice for both management and disaster readiness, and they can reduce the physical and logistical impacts of events such as a hurricane (US Department of Education 2010; UNESCO 2014). After a disaster, strong communication practices, personnel management, and community engagement can help schools reopen faster, mobilize resources to recover, and provide students needed psychosocial support (UNISDR and UNESCO 2007). Finally, well-managed schools that proactively respond to change may be more likely to learn from past shocks and adapt more effective disaster risk mitigation and preparedness practices to reduce the impacts of future shocks.[6]

To estimate how much management practices can help schools' recovery and response through the channels described above, Adelman, Baron, and Lemos (forthcoming) use variation across Haiti in schools' exposure to Matthew's intensity, coupled with multiple types of newly collected data on management practices, the hurricane's intensity and impacts, and disaster risk management practices. From April 2016 to June 2017, the authors ran four independent rounds of data to capture (a) student learning measures about five months before the hurricane using the EGRA (Early Grade Reading Assessment), (b) day-to-day management practices at the school prior to the hurricane, using the Development World Management Survey (D-WMS) and emergency response to the hurricane immediately after the shock, (c) recovery measures and adoption of disaster preparedness and mitigation practices 9 months after the hurricane using the School Disaster Management Survey (SDMS) described in the previous chapter, and (d) student learning measures and disaster management audits 9–10 months after the hurricane.

Data on both local wind speeds and individual school infrastructure damage provide measures of the impacts of Matthew on schools and show the variation across schools in the extent of Matthew's impacts. Adelman, Baron, and Lemos (forthcoming) assume that, controlling for basic school characteristics, including school size, sector, and prehurricane infrastructure quality, the intensity of exposure to the hurricane was effectively random. This assumption is supported by the fact that hurricane paths in Haiti are largely determined by global winds and other meteorological factors that change regularly, and that little information was available about the hurricane in the days leading up to its landfall. The authors provide detailed evidence to support the lack of a relationship between management quality at the school, and when the director learned about the hurricane or what the director expected in terms of its strength and potential destruction (figure 3.4).

FIGURE 3.4

Well managed and poorly managed schools in Haiti were equally likely to be surprised by the impacts of Hurricane Matthew

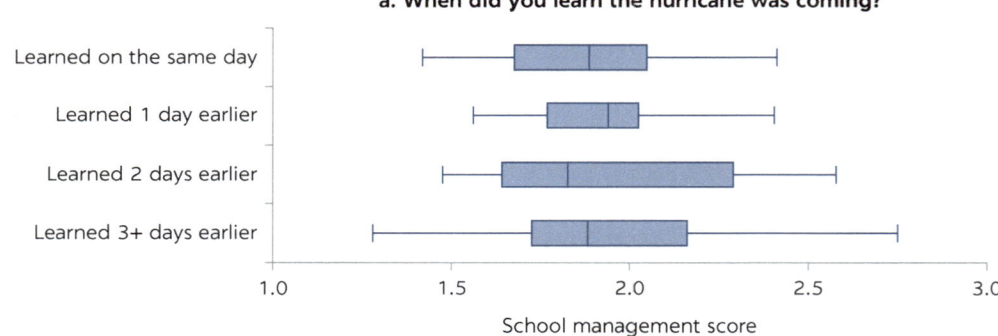

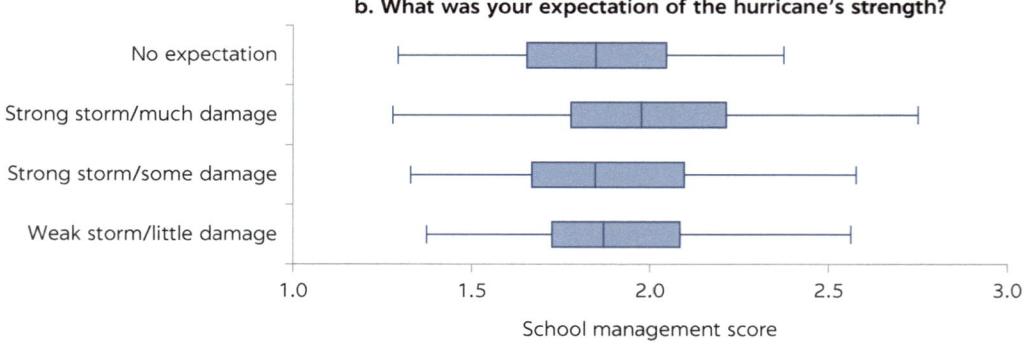

Source: Adelman, Baron, and Lemos, forthcoming.
Note: This figure shows the minimum, first quartile, median, third quartile, and maximum for the distributions of Development World Management Survey school management scores (collected before the hurricane) on the horizontal axis for each categorical response to two questions: "When did you learn the hurricane was coming?" and "What was your expectation of the hurricane's strength?" Outside values are dropped from the graph. The Development World Management Survey school management score includes survey noise controls. Number of observations: 279.

FIGURE 3.5
Better managed schools damaged by Hurricane Matthew in Haiti reopened faster and had teachers and students back sooner than poorly managed schools

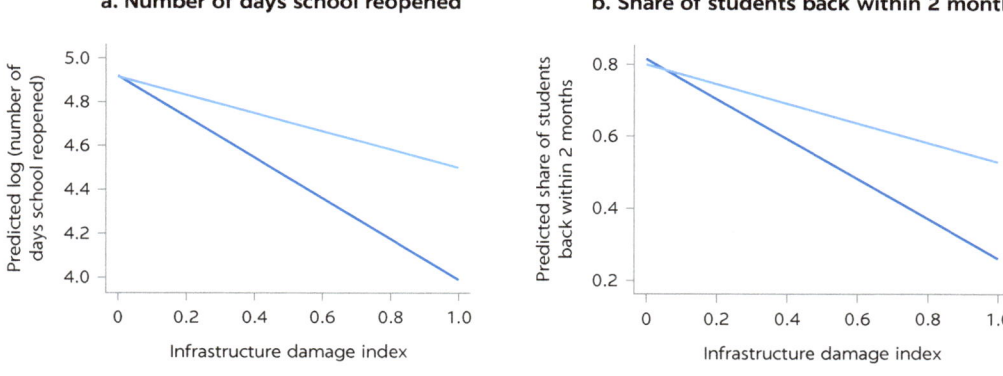

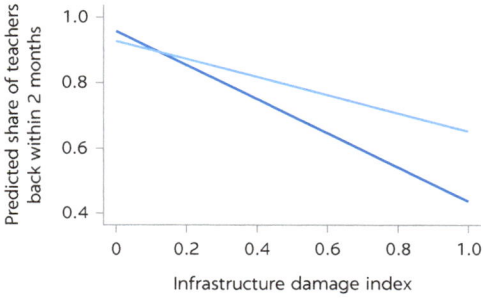

Source: Adelman, Baron, and Lemos, forthcoming.
Note: This figure shows the estimated marginal effect of damage from the hurricane in the vertical axis, as indicated by the school infrastructure damage index on the horizontal axis, on three recovery indicators measured post-hurricane: (a) number of days school reopened (in logs), (b) share of students back within two months, (c) share of teachers back within two months. For each of these recovery measures, the light blue line represents the predicted marginal effect of the hurricane for schools with high management quality (management equal or above the mean), and the dark blue line shows the effect on schools with low management quality (below the mean). These estimates come from original least squares regressions of recovery indicators on hurricane damage measures, Development World Management Survey school management scores, and a range of school characteristics (sector, size, pre-hurricane infrastructure quality), and interaction terms of damage with DWMS school management score. Number of observations: 230.

Three important results emerge from the analysis (figure 3.5). First, even with low average day-to-day management quality and limited variation, routinely better managed schools are better able to mitigate the impacts of the hurricane, controlling for a range of school characteristics and the intensity of exposure to the storm. For example, the authors show that for schools that report damage to 20 percent of the school building, 1 standard deviation better D-WMS score is associated with an increase of 5 percentage points in the share of students back within two months. Second, there is an increasing marginal effect of infrastructure damage from the hurricane on recovery indicators measured seven to eight months posthurricane. Finally, better managed schools recover faster, and this difference is more pronounced at higher levels of damage.

Better managed schools are also better able to mitigate the impacts of Matthew on student learning. For schools experiencing the highest level of infrastructure damage, 1 standard deviation of better routine management

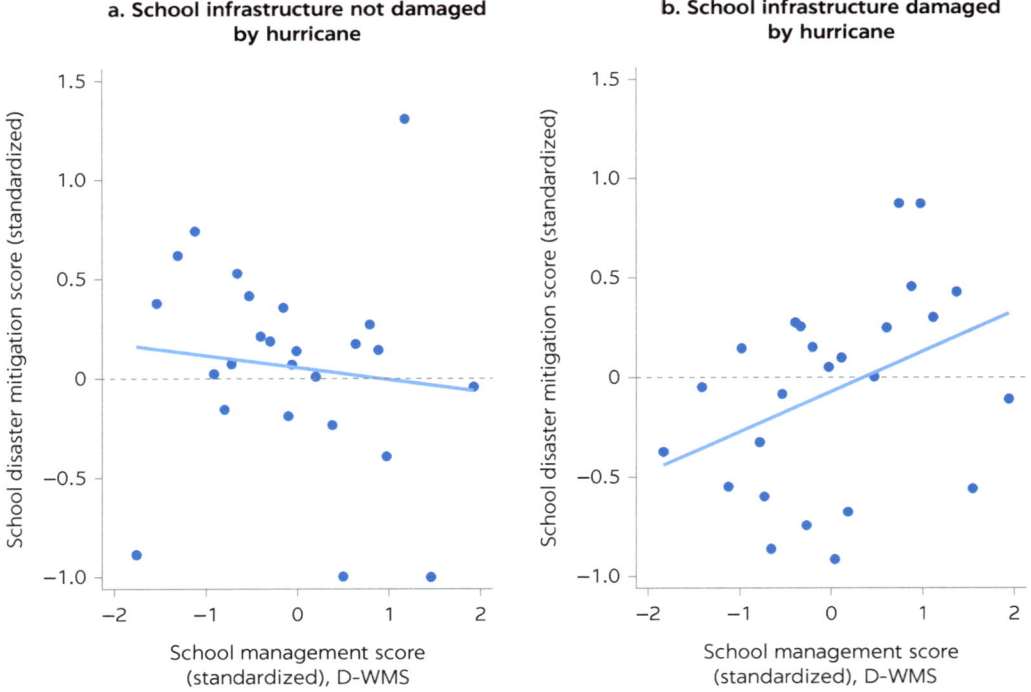

FIGURE 3.6

Better managed schools damaged by Hurricane Matthew in Haiti adopt better disaster preparedness and mitigation practices afterwards, while undamaged schools do not

Source: Adelman, Baron, and Lemos, forthcoming.
Note: This figure shows on the horizontal axis the Development World Management Survey (D-WMS) school management practices index (collected before the hurricane) and on the vertical axis the adoption of school disaster management practices index (collected 9 months after the hurricane), conditioning on a range of school and school director characteristics, wind speed, and survey noise controls for both measures. Data are plotted in 25 equal size bins of the school management practices variable. The line presents the best fit. Number of observations: 227 (schools with no infrastructure damage: 115, schools with infrastructure damage: 112).

practices would equate to a 0.43 standard deviation increase in average score on the EGRA administered at the end of the school year in which Matthew hit (approximately nine months later). Finally, schools with better routine management (as measured by the D-WMS) adopt better disaster management practices after the hurricane if they experienced infrastructure damage, conditioning on a range of school and school director characteristics. For these schools, 1 standard deviation of better routine management practices is associated with a 0.20 standard deviation improvement in newly adopted disaster management practices nine months after Matthew (figure 3.6, panel b).[7] On the other hand, schools that did not experience any damage (despite being in areas hit by the hurricane) do not seem to be adopting better practices.

New research is just beginning to emerge on managing schools through the ongoing COVID-19 pandemic, which created the large, global shock of school closures followed by an ongoing period of uncertainty. For example, Bobonis and others (2020) leverage a research program on in-service director training begun prior to the pandemic to assess the correlation between school management quality and adaptation to distance learning in Puerto Rico. Their preliminary findings show that in public schools with a

1 standard deviation higher score on the D-WMS in people management and target setting, 9.9 percent more students are actively using Puerto Rico's main online learning platform.

MANAGERS AND MANAGEMENT PRACTICES IN THE MIDDLE LAYERS

The middle layers of public systems—such as local administrative districts, central technical units, and autonomous institutes—have been understudied relative to their potential importance in shaping education outcomes and remain a critical area for further research. Recent advances in measurement of both management and bureaucratic performance in other sectors hold promise for education. Rasul and Rogger (2018), as well as Rasul, Rogger, and Williams (forthcoming), adapt the WMS instrument to measure the quality of management practices in defined units of various civil service organizations in Nigeria and Ghana, including agriculture, water, and education ministries, and exploit detailed administrative data on each unit's planned projects, execution rates, and quality of execution to create measures of unit performance.

Within both countries, they find substantial variation across units in the quality of management practices and in performance.[8] They also find strong and nuanced correlations between specific management practices and unit performance (as measured by quality-adjusted project completion). Specifically, stronger incentives and monitoring practices are negatively correlated with project completion, while stronger practices that enable autonomy for bureaucrats are positively correlated with project completion. Moreover, these relationships are dependent on other factors, including how well defined a project is. Their results point toward a rich research agenda that examines how management practices interact with the broader operating environment to determine the performance of these middle layers of public systems. In education, ongoing research across several middle-income countries will start to shed light on some of these topics, including, for example, research on the decision-making processes of local-level education officials, the effectiveness of performance incentives for staff supporting groups of schools, and the impacts of better data and management tools.[9] For example, Sabarwal, Asaduzzaman, and Ramachandran (2020) use a novel measurement strategy of "gamified vignettes" on tablets to assess the decision-making processes of district education officers across Nepal and Bangladesh. The authors find that these officers generally have beliefs and preferences that align with evidence on what works to increase learning for all, with a few critical exceptions. For example, they prioritize the demands of vocal parents over the needs of disadvantaged students, appear unwilling to sanction low-performing teachers, and are divided in terms of prioritizing equity in inputs versus equity in outcomes. These results highlight a potentially promising new approach to understanding how middle managers make decisions, in order to develop more effective means of engaging and supporting these actors. As education is among the largest sectors in terms of public spending and employment for most LAC countries, further research to understand both what determines the upstream service delivery that shapes the quality of schools, and how to improve it, are a high priority.

SYSTEM-LEVEL MANAGEMENT AND SERVICE DELIVERY

At the system level, a large body of research on the economics of education literature has provided increasingly convincing empirical evidence that, in addition to student and family background and levels of system inputs, institutional characteristics also matter for student achievement (Hanushek and Woessmann 2011; Todd and Wolpin 2003). These institutional characteristics include the allocation of responsibilities to the school level (frequently referred to as autonomy), the existence of specific practices such as external school leaving exams and in-class observation of teachers' practice (aspects of accountability), the extent of competition from the private sector, and the interactions across these features. As shown in multiple waves of international learning assessment data, school autonomy coupled with accountability as well as increased private sector competition has positive effects on educational achievement and also helps explain cross-country achievement differences above and beyond other inputs (Woessmann 2016).

Although these results provide convincing evidence on the link between institutional characteristics and achievement outcomes, moving from the insight that institutions matter to reliably predicting the effects of changing specific institutional characteristics is not straightforward.[10] For example, though measures of school autonomy are an important institutional characteristic measured in the literature, the effect of autonomy on educational achievement is neither theoretically and nor empirically straightforward.

In a model of institutional effects on education production, Bishop and Woessmann (2004) suggest that the allocation of responsibilities to officials at different levels must consider both officials' knowledge and incentives, such that different responsibilities may be optimally allocated to different levels. For example, they argue that responsibilities related to functions of curriculum and learning standards are likely better allocated to the national level to take advantage of greater centralized knowledge. In contrast, personnel-related functions may best be allocated to schools or local officials, who are able to build much richer knowledge of local needs and individuals' day-to-day job performance. Across responsibilities, Bishop and Woessmann (2004) suggest that perhaps an intermediate level of bureaucracy would represent the best tradeoff between the drawbacks of school-level and national-level allocation. Empirically, an extensive literature on system decentralization in LAC highlights the risks of increasing inequalities as the benefits of devolving responsibilities tend to accrue to local systems with great management capacity and resources (see, for example, Brutti 2020; Galiani, Gertler, and Schargrodsky 2008). Hanushek, Link, and Woessmann (2013) illustrate this at the global level by pointing out that increasing school autonomy is positively correlated with higher educational achievement only in countries with stronger overall institutions as proxied by higher GDP per capita and international assessment scores.

Yet most of the evidence on the importance of institutions mentioned above comes from a limited number of variables that describe individual institutional characteristics. Although these variables are important, both the complexity of institutional settings and lack of data collection instruments to capture this complexity have limited our understanding of how institutional changes matter for educational achievement. This challenge is not confined to education, as much of the economics and political science literature has focused either on elected politicians or frontline service providers (street-level bureaucrats) like teachers and health care workers, leaving a black box of bureaucracy in between (Finan, Olken, and Pande 2015; Pepinsky, Pierskalla, and Sacks 2017).

Adelman and others (forthcoming) attempt to address this challenge and develop new measures of the completeness, coherence, and quality of the functioning of public basic education systems. This approach draws on multiple strands of literature, including (a) functional reviews in public management (Manning and Parison 2004; Moarcas, Sondergaard, and Orbach 2011), (b) systems and state capability in public sector reform (Andrews, Pritchett, and Woolcock 2017; Pritchett 2014, 2015), and (c) the emerging data-driven literature on bureaucratic effectiveness (Hasnain and Rogger 2018; Rasul and Rogger 2018). The authors focus on specific attributes of the organizational structure, namely the allocation and execution of the tasks that make up the core functions of an education system.

To guide their data collection efforts, the authors focus on five related questions. First, are all the core functions of the education system clearly articulated and is responsibility for their execution allocated in law or regulation (de jure)? The regulatory *completeness* of responsibility allocation provides the reference point against which bureaucrats understand their roles, such that responsibilities that are not clearly allocated in regulation may not be effectively carried out, if they are carried out at all (Pritchett and Pande 2006). Second, how are responsibilities allocated across levels of education systems? This type of information, while lacking normative implications—given that optimal allocations are context dependent—can provide important insights into where decisions are being made.

Third, how aligned are the self-reports of system authorities (that is, those of a school director, her local education official, and the regulation) on the allocation of responsibilities with regulation (de jure versus de facto) and with each other? These measures of *coherence* are based on the basic managerial premise that individuals within an organization must share a common understanding of their own and each other's roles to work effectively together, which, in a public education system, would be based on regulation (Andrews and Shah 2005; Pritchett 2015).[11] Fourth, how well are functions carried out by those who are responsible? The authors use the speed of completion and outcomes (when responsibilities are carried out) to construct measures of quality of execution, which help determine the quality of education services that systems deliver (Rasul, Rogger, and Williams forthcoming; Rogger 2017). Finally, are these measures meaningful? Specifically, is coherence positively associated with education systems' quality of execution and with final outcomes in terms of student learning?

To answer these questions, as described in the previous chapter, the authors develop a new set of instruments (the Education System Coherence Survey) and apply them to the public basic education systems in four middle-income countries in Latin America: Brazil, the Dominican Republic, Guatemala, and Peru.

On the basis of this data collection exercise, the authors are able to describe a more complete picture of the management of these public education systems and provide answers to the five questions above. First, across functions, the percentage of tasks that lack a clear allocation in the legislation are not trivial, representing about 25 percent of the tasks across

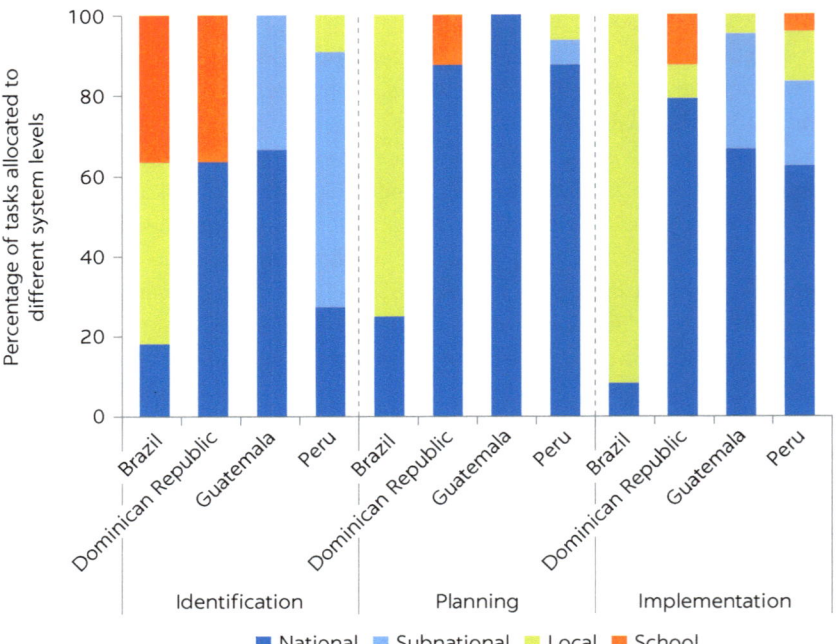

FIGURE 3.7

Substantial variation in the *de jure* allocation of tasks, and in all cases, the minority of tasks are allocated to school directors across Brazil, the Dominican Republic, Guatemala, and Peru

Source: Adelman and others, forthcoming.
Note: This figure shows the distribution of the allocation of tasks to the national, subnational, local, and school-level by dimension (monitoring and identification, planning, and implementation) and country as stated in the national legislation. The legislation review was performed by a senior analyst with familiarity with each country's education system, who allocated the primary responsibility of the tasks to an education system level according to the current legislation. Observations are at the country level, with 51 tasks by country except for Guatemala (44), where 7 of the 51 tasks are not incorporated in the legislation because of the structure of the education system.

countries (20 percent in Brazil, 29 percent in the Dominican Republic, 30 percent in Guatemala, and 24 percent in Peru).[12] Second, the allocation of tasks at the national versus more local levels varies substantially across countries, but in all cases, the minority of tasks are allocated to school directors—from under 10 percent in Guatemala, Peru, and Brazil to 18 percent in the Dominican Republic (figure 3.7). In Brazil and the Dominican Republic, the tasks allocated to school directors are concentrated in monitoring of and identification of needs, while in Guatemala and Peru no tasks are identified as being the main responsibility of school directors.

Third, although tasks for most core functions are allocated in law or regulation across countries, the coherence between this de jure allocation and bureaucrats' de facto understanding, as well as coherence between bureaucrats in their de facto understanding, varies substantially across functions and countries (figure 3.8). Across countries, education officials at the national, subnational, and local levels fail to identify 10–80 percent of tasks that are theirs according to regulation, and they claim 15–35 percent of the tasks allocated to other levels of the system. Fourth, across several functions related to the management of

FIGURE 3.8
Understanding of the *de facto* allocation of tasks across 10 core education functions shows substantial incoherence within education systems in Brazil, the Dominican Republic, Guatemala, and Peru

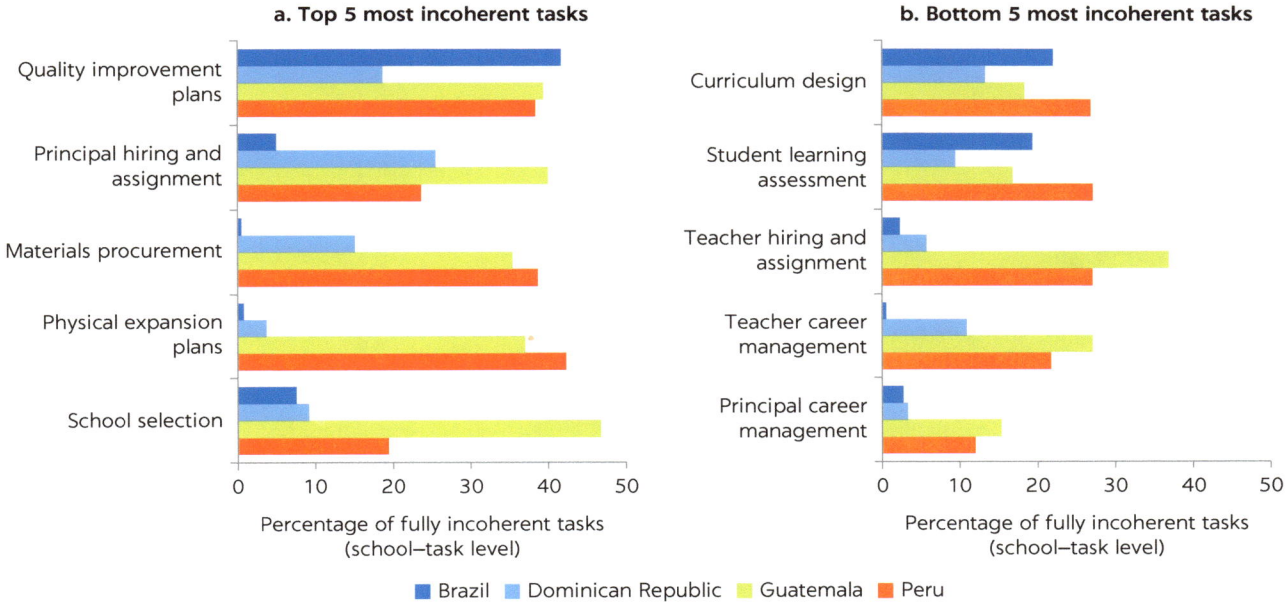

Source: Adelman and others, forthcoming.
Note: This figure shows the percentage of tasks that are fully incoherent within each education system. Full incoherence takes the value of 1 if the local official, school director, and legislation do not allocate the task to the same education system level and 0 if they do agree, fully or partially. The bar corresponds to the percentage of fully incoherent tasks by function and country. Observations are at the task level, with 51 tasks per interview. Number of school–task level observations per country: Brazil = 2,244, Dominican Republic = 4,998, Guatemala = 4,182, and Peru = 5,100.

personnel (which absorbs the bulk of most education systems' budgets), officials report incomplete or low-quality execution of tasks. For example, when asked about the last time a teaching vacancy occurred at their school, a minority of school directors across most countries reported that it was filled with a teacher possessing the appropriate skills (5 percent in Brazil, 18 percent in the Dominican Republic, 35 percent in Guatemala, and 56 percent in Peru).[13]

Finally, the authors find evidence suggesting that coherence within bureaucrats' understanding of task allocation affects the outcomes produced by public education systems. In the countries where learning data are available, the authors find that incoherence in the understanding of de facto task allocation between a school director, the local education official, and regulation is negatively correlated with average student learning outcomes at the school level, providing suggestive evidence that coherence matters for how education systems function and ultimately for student outcomes (figure 3.9).[14]

The instruments and measures Adelman and others (forthcoming) have developed may be useful as diagnostic tools to identify which system functions need further development and strengthening, and to approach some of the core service delivery challenges in education, such as personnel management, in a more systemic manner. Although systems are always in flux, this type of snapshot is useful in moving toward a deeper understanding of how institutions can influence educational achievement.

FIGURE 3.9

Negative correlation between the percentage of fully incoherent tasks and student learning at the school level in Brazil, the Dominican Republic, and Peru

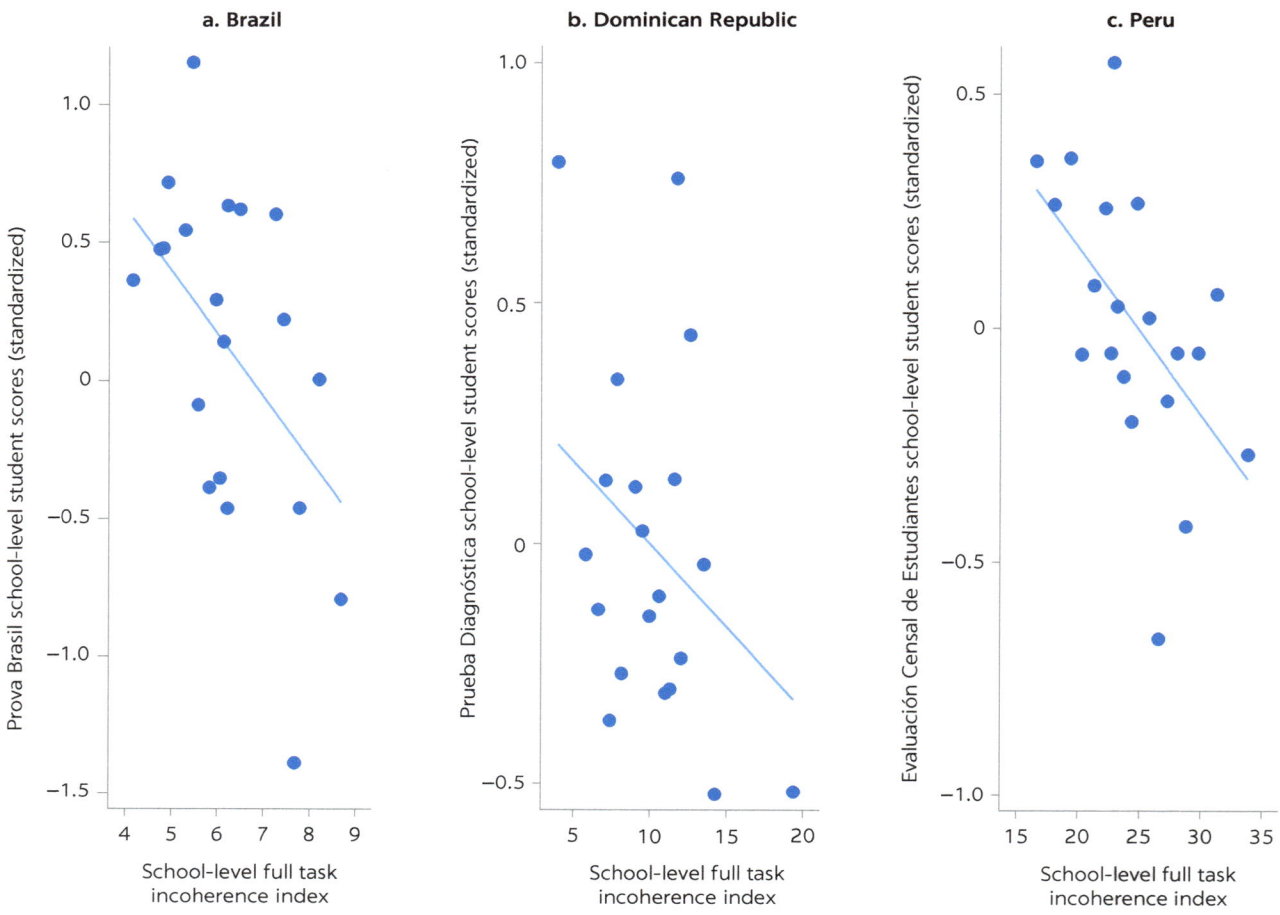

Source: Adelman and others, forthcoming.
Note: This figure shows on the horizontal axis the school-level full incoherence index—that is, the average percentage of incoherent tasks for schools in Brazil, the Dominican Republic, and Peru. Full incoherence takes the value of 1 if the local official, school director, and legislation do not allocate the task to the same education system level and 0 if they do agree, fully or partially. On the vertical axis, the figure shows school-level student achievement data from national learning assessments in each country. Portuguese and math scores of fifth graders from Prova Brasil 2015 for Brazil, Spanish and math scores of third graders from the Prueba Diagnóstica 2017 in the Dominican Republic, and Spanish and math scores of fourth graders from the Evaluación Censal de Estudiantes 2016 in Peru. Student achievement data for Guatemala is not available. A range of school, municipality, and survey noise controls are included. Data are plotted in 20 equal size bins. The line presents the best fit. Number of observations (schools): Brazil = 27, Dominican Republic = 75, and Peru = 184.

NOTES

1. Brazil, Canada, India, Sweden, the United Kingdom, and the United States.
2. This focus on selection and incentives is in keeping with the traditional focus of the personnel economics literature and related applications in public service delivery (Ashraf and others 2020; Besley 2004; Muralidharan and Sundararaman 2011).
3. Literature on teacher incentives has focused on variations in the mechanism and design of financial compensation (such as pay-per-performance or pay-per-percentile) and primarily looks at pecuniary benefits of improving performance. The novel aspect of Leaver, Lemos, and Scur's (2019) model is that it looks at teacher compensation schemes in terms of utility (including pay) but also looks at other potential aspects that matter to teachers, such as workplace organization. This expanded definition of teacher compensation may help in the interpretation of the impacts (or lack thereof) of changes to financial incentives,

as recent evidence from Pakistan and Indonesia shows that large changes in teachers' pay does not appear to affect their performance (Bau and Das 2020; de Ree and others 2018).
4. This finding is reinforced in a vastly different context in Lemos, Muralidharan, and Scur (2021), who also decompose management into operations and people practices and study their relationship with productivity across public schools and low-cost private schools in rural Andhra Pradesh, India. Private schools are better managed relative to public schools, mainly because of differences in people management, and this matters for student value added and teacher practices. They also show evidence that better people management practices at private schools (but not public) are associated both with paying higher wages to better teachers as well as keeping better teachers and letting go of worse teachers.
5. In the literature on private sector firms, different management characteristics and practices have been shown to affect firms' responses to shocks. Decentralization structure (Aghion and others 2021), risk management prior to a disaster (Collier and others 2020), and managers' handling of shocks through reoptimization of worker-task matching (Adhavaryu, Kala, and Nyshadham 2019) have proved significant in determining how shocks affect a firm's outcomes and productivity, as well as its recovery.
6. Continuous improvement, whereby problems are actively identified and resolved, is one of the key management processes measured in schools using the World Management Survey (Lemos and Scur 2016). Evidence from school systems globally suggests that adoption of disaster management practices is contingent on experiencing a disaster (BRI and GRIPS 2007). Together these results suggest that most schools are unlikely to have disaster management practices in place prior to a major shock, and that better managed schools (or school systems) would be more likely to adopt such practices after a shock.
7. This correlation is significant at the 5 percent level. For schools with no damage, a 1 standard deviation of better routine management practices is associated with an insignificant −0.6 standard deviation reduction in newly adopted disaster management practices.
8. The authors restrict their comparisons to units executing projects of the same type, such as borehole-drilling projects or staff training projects.
9. The research projects mentioned are funded by the Results in Education for All Children (REACH) fund managed by the World Bank: https://www.worldbank.org/en/programs/reach.
10. See Pande and Udry (2005) for a relevant discussion of these challenges in the growth literature.
11. Within Pritchett's 2015 framework, the proposed measure of coherence in Adelman and others (forthcoming) approximately corresponds to a detailed measure of the delegation element within the management relationship.
12. Clarity of allocation in legislation was assessed as follows: two education experts (who were not familiar with the legislation of any of the countries) were asked to review the information provided in the legislative review separately and indicate when responsibility for a particular task was not assigned or was ambiguous. Tasks that both education experts indicated as ambiguous or unassigned were classified as lacking a clear allocation in the legislation.
13. These measures indicate low-quality execution of the task, but they do not pinpoint the root causes. For example, failure to appropriately fill teaching vacancies could the result of a weak pool of potential new hires, ineffective hiring practices, or ineffective assignment practices.
14. Given the relatively small sample size and correlational nature of the relationship, these results are suggestive and additional research is needed in this area.

REFERENCES

Adelman, Melissa, Juan Baron, and Renata Lemos. Forthcoming. "Managing Shocks in Education: Evidence from Hurricane Matthew in Haiti." Working paper, World Bank, Washington, DC.

Adelman, Melissa, Peter Holland, and Tillmann Heidelk. 2017. "Increasing Access by Waiving Tuition: Evidence from Haiti." *Comparative Education Review* 61 (4): 804–31.

Adelman, Melissa, Renata Lemos, Reema Nayar, and Maria Jose Vargas. Forthcoming. "(In)coherence in the Management of Education Systems in Latin America." Working paper, World Bank, Washington, DC.

Adhavaryu, Achyuta, Namrata Kala, and Anant Nyshadham. 2019. "Management and Shocks to Worker Productivity." NBER Working Papers 25865, National Bureau of Economic Research. Cambridge, MA.

Aghion, Philippe, Nicholas Bloom, Brian Lucking, Raffaella Sadun, and John Van Reenen. 2021. "Turbulence, Firm Decentralization, and Growth in Bad Times." *American Economic Journal: Applied Economics* 13 (1): 133–69.

Andrews, Matt, Lant Pritchett, and Michael Woolcock. 2017. *Building State Capability: Evidence, Analysis, Action*. New York: Oxford University Press.

Andrews, Matthew, and Anwar Shah. 2005. "Citizen-Centered Governance: A New Approach to Public Sector Reform." In *Public Expenditure Analysis*, edited by A. Shah, 153–82. Washington, DC: World Bank.

Ashraf, Nava, Oriana Bandiera, Edward Davenport, and Scott Lee. 2020. "Losing Prosociality in the Quest for Talent? Sorting, Selection, and Productivity in the Delivery of Public Services." *American Economic Review* 110 (5): 1355–94.

Archibong, Belinda, and Francis Annan. 2020. "Schooling in Sickness and in Health: The Effects of Epidemic Disease on Gender Inequality." Working paper, Barnard College.

Bandiera, Oriana, Niklas Buehren, Markus Goldstein, Imran Rasul, and Andrea Smurra. 2020. "Do School Closures during an Epidemic Have Persistent Effects? Evidence from Sierra Leone in the Time of Ebola." Working paper, UCL.

Bau, Natalie, and Jishnu Das. 2020. "Teacher Value Added in a Low-Income Country." *American Economic Journal: Economic Policy* 12 (1): 62–96.

Beg, Sabrin, Anne Fitzpatrick, and Adrienne M. Lucas. 2021. "Gender Bias in Assessments of Teacher Performance." *American Economic Association: Papers & Proceedings*.

Besley, Timothy. 2004. "Paying Politicians: Theory and Evidence." *Journal of the European Economic Association* 2 (2–3): 193–215.

Bishop, John H., and Ludger Woessmann. 2004. "Institutional Effects in a Simple Model of Educational Production." *Education Economics* 12 (1): 17–38.

Bloom, Nicholas, Renata Lemos, Raffaella Sadun, and John Van Reenen. 2015. "Does Management Matter in Schools?" *The Economic Journal* 125 (584): 647–74.

Bobonis, Gustavo, Marco Gonzalez-Navarro, Daniela Scur, and Jessica Wagner. 2020. "Management Practices and Coordination of Responses to COVID-19 in Public Schools: Evidence from Puerto Rico." University of Toronto Mimeo.

Branch, Gregory F., Eric A. Hanushek, and Steven G. Rivkin. 2012. "Estimating the Effect of Leaders on Public Sector Productivity: The Case of School Principals." NBER Working Paper 17803, National Bureau of Economic Research, Cambridge, MA.

Brutti, Zelda. 2020. "Cities Drifting Apart: Heterogeneous Outcomes of Decentralizing Public Education." *IZA Journal of Labor Economics* 9: 3.

BRI (Building Research Institute) and GRIPS (National Graduate Institute for Policy Studies). 2007. "Disaster Education." https://www.preventionweb.net/files/3442_Disaster Education.pdf.

Chakrabarti, Rajashri, Max Livingston, and Elizabeth Setren. 2015. "The Great Recession's Impact on School District Finances in New York State." *FRBNY Economic Policy Review*.

Collier, Benjamin L., Andrew F. Haughwout, Howard C. Kunreuther, and Erwann O. Michel. Kerjan, 2020. "Firms' Management of Infrequent Shocks." *Journal of Money, Credit, and Banking* 52 (6): 1329–59.

Deming, David, and Christopher Walters. 2017. "The Impact of Price Caps and Spending Cuts on US Postsecondary Attainment." NBER Working Paper 23736, National Bureau of Economic Research, Cambridge, MA.

de Ree, Joppe, Karthik Muralidharan, Menno Pradhan, and Halsey Rogers. 2018. "Double for Nothing? Experimental Evidence on an Unconditional Teacher Salary Increase in Indonesia." *Quarterly Journal of Economics* 133 (2): 993–1039.

DiPietro, Giorgio. 2018. "The Academic Impact of Natural Disasters: Evidence from L'Aquila Earthquake." *Education Economics* 26 (1): 62–77.

Finan, Frederico, Benjamin Olken, and Rohini Pande. 2015. "The Personnel Economics of the State." NBER Working Paper 21825, National Bureau of Economic Research, Cambridge, MA.

Galiani, Sebastian, Paul Gertler, and Ernesto Schargrodsky. 2008. "School Decentralization: Helping the Good Get Better, but Leaving the Poor Behind." *Journal of Public Economics* 92 (10–11): 2106–120.

Gould, Eric, Victor Lavy, and Daniele Paserman. 2009. "Does Immigration Affect the Long-Term Educational Outcomes of Natives? Quasi-Experimental Evidence." *The Economic Journal* 119 (540): 1243–69.

Grissom, Jason, and Brendan Bartanen. 2019. "Strategic Retention: Principal Effectiveness and Teacher Turnover in Multiple-Measure Teacher Evaluation Systems." *American Educational Research Journal* 56 (2): 514–55.

Grissom, Jason, Demetra Kalogrides, and Susanna Loeb. 2017. "Strategic Staffing? How Performance Pressures Affect the Distribution of Teachers within Schools and Resulting Student Achievement." *American Educational Research Journal* 54 (6): 1079–116.

Grissom, Jason, and Susanna Loeb. 2011. "Triangulating Principal Effectiveness: How Perspectives of Parents, Teachers, and Assistant Principals Identify the Central Importance of Managerial Skills." *American Educational Research Journal* 48 (5): 1091–123.

Grissom, Jason, Susanna Loeb, and Benjamin Master. 2013. "Effective Instructional Time Use for School Leaders: Longitudinal Evidence from Observations of Principals." *Educational Researcher* 42 (8): 433–44.

Gutmann, Ethan, Roy Rasmussen, Changhai Liu, Kyoko Ikeda, Cindy Bruyere, James Done, Luca Garre, Peter Frijs-Hansen, and Vidyunmala Veldore. 2018. "Changes in Hurricanes from a 13-Year Convection-Permitting Pseudo-Global Warming Simulation." *Journal of Climate* 31 (9): 3643–57.

Hanushek, Eric, Susanne Link, and Ludger Woessmann. 2013. "Does School Autonomy Make Sense Everywhere? Panel Estimates from PISA." *Journal of Development Economics* 104: 2012–32.

Hanushek, Eric, and Ludger Woessmann. 2011. "The Economics of International Differences in Educational Achievement." In *Handbook of the Economics of Education*, edited by E. A. Hanushek, S. Machin, and L. Woessmann (vol. 3), 89–200. North Holland, Amsterdam.

Hasnain, Zahid, and Daniel Rogger. 2018. "Innovating Bureaucracy for Increasing Government Productivity" (brief). World Bank, Washington, DC. http://documents.worldbank.org/curated/en/661371552669784935/Innovating-Bureaucracy-for-Increasing-Government-Productivity.

Jackson, C. Kirabo, Cora Wigger, and Heyu Xiong. 2018. "Do School Spending Cuts Matter? Evidence from the Great Recession." NBER Working Paper 24203, National Bureau of Economic Research, Cambridge, MA.

Kraft, Matthew, William Marinell, and Darrick Shen-Wei Yee. 2016. "School Organizational Contexts, Teacher Turnover, and Student Achievement: Evidence from Panel Data." *American Educational Research Journal* 53 (5): 1411–49.

Ladd, Helen. 2011. "Teachers' Perceptions of Their Working Conditions: How Predictive of Planned and Actual Teacher Movement?" *Educational Evaluation and Policy Analysis* 33 (2): 235–61.

Leaver, Clare, Renata Lemos, and Daniela Scur. 2019. "Measuring and Explaining Management in Schools: New Approaches Using Public Data." Policy Research Working Paper 9053, World Bank, Washington, DC.

Lemos, Renata, Karthik Muralidharan, and Daniela Scur (2021). "Personnel Management and School Productivity: Evidence from India." NBER Working Paper 28336, National Bureau of Economic Research, Cambridge, MA.

Lemos, Renata, and Daniela Scur. 2016. "Developing Management: An Expanded Evaluation Tool for Developing Countries." RISE Working Paper 16/007. Oxford: Research on Improving Systems of Education (RISE).

Li, Xuan. 2018. "The Costs of Workplace Favoritism: Evidence from Promotions in Chinese High Schools." Columbia University Mimeo.

Loeb, Susanna, Demetra Kalogrides, and Tara Béteille. 2012. "Effective Schools: Teacher Hiring, Assignment, Development, and Retention." *Education Finance and Policy* 7 (3): 269–304.

Manning, Nick, and Neil Parison. 2004. *International Public Administration Reform: Implications for the Russian Federation*. Directions in Development. Washington, DC: World Bank.

Moarcas, Mariana, Lars Sondergaard, and Eliezer Orbach. 2011. "Romania—Functional Review: Pre-University Education Sector: Main Report." World Bank, Washington, DC. http://documents.worldbank.org/curated/en/473931468092366883/Main-report

Muralidharan, Karthik, and Venkatesh Sundararaman. 2011. "Teacher Performance Pay: Experimental Evidence from India." *Journal of Political Economy* 119 (1): 39–77.

NOAA (National Oceanic and Atmospheric Administration). 2018. "Global Warming and Hurricanes: An Overview of Current Research Results." https://www.gfdl.noaa.gov/global-warming-and-hurricanes/.

Pande, Rohini, and Christopher Udry. 2005. "Institutions and Development: A View from Below." Economic Growth Center Discussion Paper 928, Yale University, New Haven, CT.

Papay, John, Eric Taylor, John Tyler, and Mary Laski. 2020. "Learning Job Skills from Colleagues at Work: Evidence from a Field Experiment using Teacher Performance Data." *American Economic Journal: Economic Policy* 12 (1): 359–88.

Pepinsky, Thomas, Jan Pierskalla, and Audrey Sacks. 2017. "Bureaucracy and Service Delivery." *Annual Review of Political Science* 20: 249–68.

Pritchett, Lant. 2014. "The Risks to Education Systems from Design Mismatch and Global Isomorphism." Working Paper No. 277, Center for International Development at Harvard University, Cambridge, MA.

Pritchett, Lant. 2015. "Creating Education Systems Coherent for Learning Outcomes: Making the Transition from Schooling to Learning." RISE Working Paper 15/005. Oxford: Research on Improving Systems of Education (RISE).

Pritchett, Lant, and Varad Pande. 2006. *Making Primary Education Work for India's Rural Poor: A Proposal for Effective Decentralization*. Social Development—South Asia Series Paper No. 95. Washington, DC: World Bank.

Rasul, Imran, and Daniel Rogger. 2018. "Management of Bureaucrats and Public Service Delivery: Evidence from the Nigerian Civil Service." *The Economic Journal* 128 (608): 413–46.

Rasul, Imran, Daniel Rogger, and Martin Williams. Forthcoming. "Management, Organizational Performance, and Task Clarity: Evidence from Ghana's Civil Service." *Journal of Public Administration Research and Theory*.

Rogger, Daniel. 2017. "Who Serves the Poor? Surveying Civil Servants in the Developing World." Policy Research Working Paper 8051, World Bank, Washington, DC.

Sabarwal, Shwetlena, T. M. Asaduzzaman, and Deepika Ramachandran. 2020. "Managing the Middle: Decision-Making Within Education Bureaucracies." Working Paper, World Bank, Washington, DC.

Sebastian, James, and Elaine Allensworth. 2012. "The Influence of Principal Leadership on Classroom Instruction and Student Learning: A Study of Mediated Pathways to Learning." *Educational Administration Quarterly* 48 (4): 626–63.

Stockard, Jean, and Michael Lehman. 2004. "Influences on the Satisfaction and Retention of 1st-Year Teachers: The Importance of Effective School Management." *Educational Administration Quarterly* 40 (5): 742–71.

Taylor, Eric, and John Tyler. 2012. "The Effect of Evaluation on Teacher Performance." *American Economic Review* 102 (7): 3628–651.

Todd, Petra, and Kenneth Wolpin. 2003. "On the Specification and Estimation of the Production Function for Cognitive Achievement." *The Economic Journal* 113 (485): F3–F33.

US Department of Education, Office of Safe and Drug-Free Schools. 2007. *Practical Information on Crisis Planning. A Guide for Schools and Communities*. Washington, DC: US Department of Education.

US Department of Education, Office of Safe and Drug-Free Schools. 2010. *Action Guide for Emergency Management at Institutions of Higher Education*. Washington, DC: US Department of Education.

UNESCO (United Nations Educational, Scientific and Cultural Organization). 2014. "A Teacher's Guide to Disaster Risk Reduction. Stay Safe and Be Prepared." Paris: UNESCO.

UNICEF ROSA (United Nations Children's Fund Regional Office for South Asia). 2006. *Education in Emergencies. A Resource Tool Kit*. Kathmandu, Nepal: Regional Office for South Asia in Conjunction with New York Headquarters.

UNISDR (United Nations International Strategy for Disaster Reduction) and UNESCO (UN Educational, Scientific and Cultural Organization). 2007. *Towards a Culture of Prevention: Disaster Risk Reduction Begins at School—Good Practices and Lessons Learned*. Geneva: UNISDR. https://www.unisdr.org/files/761_education-good-practices.pdf.

Woessmann, Ludger. 2016. "The Importance of School Systems: Evidence from International Differences in Student Achievement." *Journal of Economic Perspectives* 30 (3): 3–32.

World Bank. 2013. *World Development Report 2014: Risk and Opportunity-Managing Risk for Development*. Washington, DC: World Bank.

World Bank. 2018. *World Development Report 2018: Learning to Realize Education's Promise*. Washington, DC: World Bank.

4 How to Improve Education Management in LAC

Given the evidence presented in the previous chapters on how management matters for education outcomes and how to measure it, this chapter explores questions of how to improve management in Latin America and the Caribbean (LAC) and how much such improvements can affect student outcomes. Broadly speaking, at least three approaches are used for improving management in schools, the middle layers above the school level, and education systems more broadly. These approaches include selecting managers differently; creating or improving management training, support, and incentives; and aligning actors in the system toward better management. This chapter reviews a small but growing literature that attempts to rigorously evaluate these approaches, with a focus on several new empirical studies from LAC. The evidence so far points to solutions that are neither cheap nor easy but that hold promise for improving management practices and school outcomes.

STRENGTHENING SELECTION PROCESSES FOR SCHOOL DIRECTORS

The quality of management practices depends heavily on the quality of the public sector managers who implement them. In fact, a sizable descriptive literature on high-performing education systems around the world stresses the importance of purposefully developing talent for managerial positions, including school directors, through early leadership experiences and induction training and mentoring programs, coupled with highly meritocratic selection mechanisms (Barber, Whelan, and Clark 2010; Jensen, Downing, and Clark 2017).

In these high-performing systems, however, at least two underlying factors appear to be crucial, and they may not be as well-developed in LAC or other regions. First is a high-quality pool of candidates. In nearly all high-performing systems, teachers—the pool from which directors and many education managers are initially drawn—are an already highly selected population with strong training and skills, yet this is not the case in much of LAC (Bruns and Luque 2015). The second factor is a strong and common understanding among those involved in the selection process of what to look for in applicants. As detailed in

Barber, Whelan, and Clark (2010) high-performing systems primarily use interviews, presentations, and recommendations from colleagues and supervisors as inputs to the selection process, in effect relying heavily on the judgment of system actors (whether it be school boards, superintendents, or other selection panels). In countries where those actors have diverging views or have different incentives for identifying management talent, implementing such selection mechanisms may at first yield unexpected results; the approach may take significant time to evolve into a well-functioning system. More generally, high-performing systems offer important experiences on manager selection, but these experiences do not automatically translate into applicable evidence outside of their particular contexts (Andrews, Pritchett, and Woolcock 2017; Pritchett and Woolcock 2004).

Outside of education, a nascent literature on personnel economics in developing countries points to two additional insights regarding selection of bureaucrats (including directors and other education managers). First, higher wages and better career advancement prospects can be effective in attracting a higher-quality applicant pool (as measured by cognitive and socioemotional assessments and on-the-job performance) and in increasing job acceptance rates (Ashraf, and others 2020; Dal Bó, Finan, and Rossi 2013). However, given the political economy of public education in most countries, higher wages are almost always applied to incumbents as well, implying significant increases in public expenditures for a slowly changing stock of service providers, making this option less likely to be cost-effective (de Ree and others 2018). Second, we still know relatively little about how different screening mechanisms affect who applies in the first place and the traits of who is selected, for example, whether screening beyond technical skills (such as for prosocial motivation, honesty, or other personality traits) is desirable or even feasible in many developing country contexts (Finan, Olken, and Pande 2015).

For school directors and other managers, these results suggest that changes in selection mechanisms should be studied carefully, to better understand the impacts they have on the traits and performance of those who enter the system. In LAC, selection methods for school directors at the primary level are quite varied, as presented in chapter 2. Yet what most LAC countries do have in common is that a large percentage of school directors did not obtain their positions on the basis of demonstrated managerial skills or management potential. This presents an important opportunity for improving management at the school level, which several countries have begun working on. Ongoing research into such major policy changes sheds light on the effectiveness of newly adopted selection methods across three LAC countries: Brazil, Chile, and Peru.

To estimate the effects of selection mechanism on school directors' characteristics and ultimately on student achievement, Pereda and others (2020) focus on changes in regulations for the selection of school director that have occurred across Brazilian states since the mid-2000s. Several states passed laws mandating changes in the selection process for school directors, from appointment mechanisms in which politicians or politically elected bureaucrats appointed directors, to a range of other mechanisms, including (a) direct elections by the school community, in which parents, teachers, and sometimes students hold voting rights; (b) public examinations; (c) assessment by technical bureaucrats; and (d) combinations of these different processes. The scale of this movement is relatively unique in Latin America, with over 35 percent of current public primary school directors chosen by community election.[1] Utilizing panel data on state-run schools across Brazil, Pereda and others (2020) find that schools with directors who are selected by any of the mechanisms that use community election or technical screening (including examinations and assessment) have higher student achievement indicators. The authors present results suggesting that this relationship is explained by a management quality effect, by which directors who are directly elected or technically screened stay longer in their positions and focus more on in-service professional development for their teachers, characteristics that are both strongly correlated with student achievement. These results are in line with other recent work that finds that politically driven turnover of school staff in Brazil reduces student learning (Akhtari and others forthcoming).

Although these studies provide evidence that political appointments are a suboptimal mechanism for selecting school leaders, they are not able to answer the broader question of which selection mechanisms are optimal in different contexts—for example, whether technical screening processes outperform direct elections, and under what circumstances.[2] Two other studies provide insights on different selection mechanisms and different contexts.

Muñoz and Prem (2020) look at a new mechanism introduced by a 2011 reform in Chile to select school directors. Before 2011, the selection of directors to public schools was the sole responsibility of municipalities and therefore was not supervised by the central government. After the reform, directors could be elected through public, transparent competitions in a process that is led by a third-party human resources firm. This process is supervised by the Civil Service Agency at the central level, but schools ultimately are the ones making the decision on when to switch to this new mechanism (the replacement of directors was not mandatory during the period examined, 2012 to 2016). Thus the adoption of this new mechanism was staggered, with the number of directors being elected under the new regime increasing over time.

Muñoz and Prem (2020) exploit the timing of adoption of this new selection mechanism to study its impact on director effectiveness through a staggered difference-in-differences approach.[3] They show that the effect of the new selection mechanism was positive and statistically significant, increasing director effectiveness by approximately .04 standard deviations and remaining stable over time (figure 4.1). Despite being modest in magnitude, these results are very promising, suggesting that the roll-out of such policies can be successful over time in attracting and retaining good candidates in government positions offering rigid wage structures, such as the post of school director in many countries.

Another country that has made substantial progress in reforming their director selection process is Peru. Using different approaches than those in Brazil and Chile, Peru's reform was coordinated and implemented at the central level or through strict central-level oversight. In 2014 the central government introduced a merit-based civil service examination combined with a revised compensation package for accessing school managerial positions, essentially eliminating manager selection by local authorities. Up until then, despite existing legislation providing guidance on how to recruit school directors, they were in fact appointed locally based on a variety of factors that were not always related to merit. The new selection process, on the other hand, was first implemented through a one-time national-level examination required for all existing directors to determine whether they would be ratified in their posts or return to teaching positions, followed by an optional entrance examination for all eligible public sector teachers to fill any posts that had been opened through the first examination and any remaining vacancies in other schools.

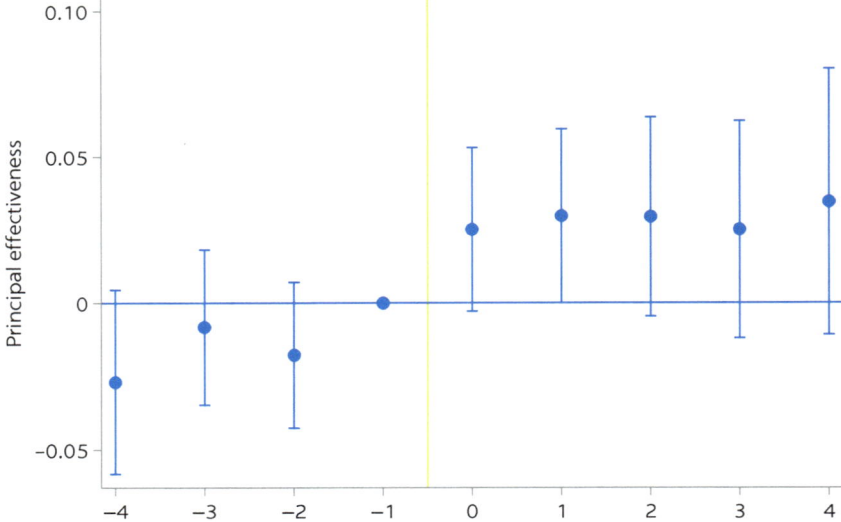

FIGURE 4.1

Small yet stable positive impact of switching from municipal appointments to civil service examinations for school directors in Chile

Source: Muñoz and Prem 2020.
Note: This figure shows the impact of the new selection system, which consisted of public, transparent competition through civil service examinations supervised by the government, the Alta Dirección Pública, on the effectiveness of public schools' directors. It plots the point estimates and 95 percent confidence intervals estimated from equation (8) in Muñoz and Prem (2020). It considers school and year fixed effects and also controls by school and municipality characteristics during the prereform period (measured in 2010), interacted with year dummies. Number of schools = 3,167.

In this context, Lemos and Piza (forthcoming) ask whether the effect of policies designed and implemented at the national level can strengthen school director selection and consequently improve student learning. First, the authors find that there was full compliance with the legislation from administering the examination to determining job offers based on their results, and also find approximately 90 percent compliance in accepting the results of the examination through ratification and job offers by school directors, suggesting that there is potential for successful implementation of such large-scale reforms.

Second, to estimate the impact on learning, Lemos and Piza (forthcoming) compare schools where the director failed the examination and should have been replaced (treated schools) with schools where directors passed and should have retained their post (nontreated schools). They use a differences-in-differences approach with propensity score weighting with school-level standardized student examinations, as well as a value added model using matched student examination data across years. Surprisingly, the authors find that the immediate impact of the reform on school performance in math and reading was negative (approximately 0.10 standard deviations). When exploring heterogeneous effects on the basis of school location to understand whether the policy produced differential effects on students across the country, given the large scale of the reform, the authors find that these results are mostly driven by schools in rural areas. In fact, the reform seems to have had a short-term yet persistent reduction of between 0.1 to 0.2 standard deviations in school performance in rural areas, whereas the effect was null in urban areas (figure 4.2). Interestingly, the authors

FIGURE 4.2
Introduction of sit-in examination to select school directors in Peru had a short-term yet persistent negative impact on student value added across multiple cohorts in rural schools, but not in urban schools

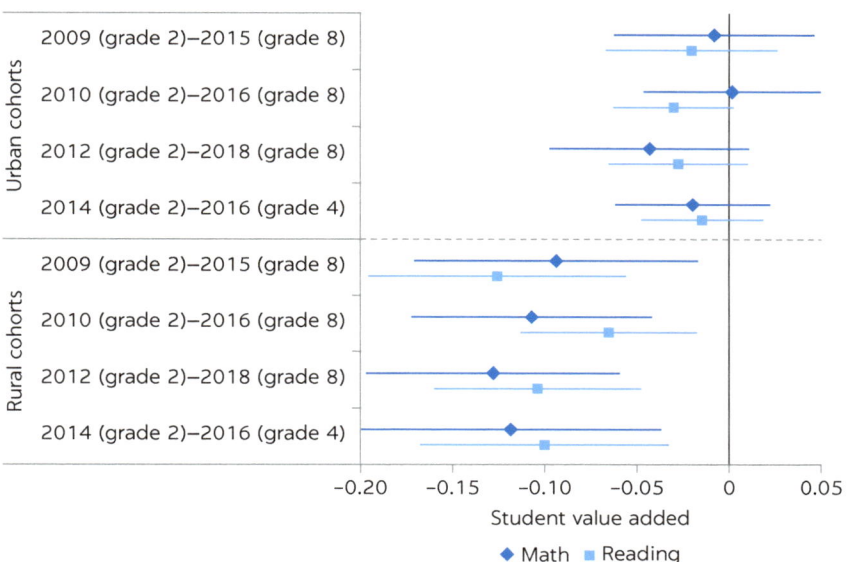

Source: World Bank calculations based on data from Lemos and Piza, forthcoming.
Note: This figure shows the intention-to-treat effect of implementing sit-in examinations to select school directors in Peru on student value added. It plots the point estimate and 95 percent confidence intervals from individual regressions using a student value added model. Student value added is available for four cohorts: three cohorts are observed in grade 2 in years 2009, 2010, and 2012 and again in grade 8 six years later in years 2015, 2016, 2018, and one cohort is observed in grade 2 in year 2014 and grade 4 two years later in 2016. All specifications include controls for log of number of students in school and a dummy for multigrade teaching. Number of schools = 6,482; number of students = 330,302.

show that these results in student learning are not driven by student composition effects, that is, there were no substantial differences in dropouts or grade promotion between the treated and nontreated groups within both rural and urban areas.

Given such differences within the treated and nontreated groups in rural versus urban schools, Lemos and Piza (forthcoming) explore potential mechanisms that could explain these results. They suggest that the negative effect in rural but not urban schools might, at least partly, be driven by (a) lower supply of candidates (less competition for jobs) in rural treated schools relative to urban treated schools, as well as smaller skill gains by directors in treated versus nontreated schools within rural versus urban areas; and (b) poorer time management in rural treated schools relative to rural nontreated schools (with no differences seen between treated and nontreated schools in urban areas). These findings highlight the importance of considering the local context in the design of national education personnel policies. Using these results, the Peruvian government is introducing a new career path for directors in rural schools to close the rural-urban gap and improve its director selection mechanism. These are important lessons from the region as other countries in LAC—such as the Dominican Republic[4]—attempt to move to merit-based mechanisms for selecting school directors.

PROVIDE TRAINING, SUPPORT, AND INCENTIVES

As with selection methods, there is very limited well-identified evidence on the effects, and cost-effectiveness, of creating or adjusting training programs or incentive mechanisms for school directors and other education managers. Several studies describe the outcomes of preservice, induction, and in-service director training programs but cannot disentangle the effects of selection into different programs and jobs from the effects of the programs themselves (see, for example, Corcoran, Schwartz, and Weinstein 2012). Fryer (2017) provides causal estimates of an in-service training program for school directors on student outcomes. He studies the effects of an intensive two-year program that provides 300 hours of summer training and ongoing coaching, as well as tools, to a randomly selected group of directors of public elementary, middle, and high schools in Houston, Texas. The program focuses on strengthening instructional planning, data-driven instruction, and observation and feedback of classroom practices, drawing from the well-known educational leadership book *Leverage Leadership* and from the World Management Survey. Fryer finds that assignment to the training group led to a 0.19 standard deviation increase in low-stakes test scores after the first year (and 0.10 standard deviation increase in high-stakes test scores), which diminishes to zero in the second year as a result of director turnover. However, for directors who stay in their positions and implement the program with higher fidelity, effects are 0.35 standard deviations by the end of the second year. In fact, the study points to other important differences in director characteristics: the program had the greatest impacts on student learning for schools where directors are smarter, are younger, and have higher internal locus of control (sense of personal responsibility) and higher grit (perseverance and passion) (figure 4.3).[5] This suggests that despite a program being well designed, focused, and intense, its impact can still vary substantially across those who are trained. Yet, because directors oversee relatively large numbers of students, the marginal cost per student is relatively low, and the results imply one of the highest internal rates of return for an education intervention calculated to date using experimental data (Fryer 2017).

Although these results are certainly a cause for optimism and an important piece of evidence that school management training programs can have a meaningful effect on learning, it is important to interpret them with caution when considering policy implications for countries in LAC for two main reasons. First, as detailed in chapter 2, many large-scale government-supported school management training programs in LAC focus on a much wider range of management practices delivered in less time: the average program content covers 16 out of 25 practices measured by the World Management Survey in 278 hours. As a comparison, the intervention in Fryer (2017) consisted of training on three specific management practices in a similar, extended period of time (300 hours), which likely allowed for a substantially deeper understanding of how to adopt, use, and monitor these practices in the school. Second, the comparable median program cost per manager in the programs surveyed in LAC is approximately US$7,100,

FIGURE 4.3
Management training program increases student learning more in schools with directors who are smarter, younger, and with a higher sense of responsibility and perseverance in Houston, Texas

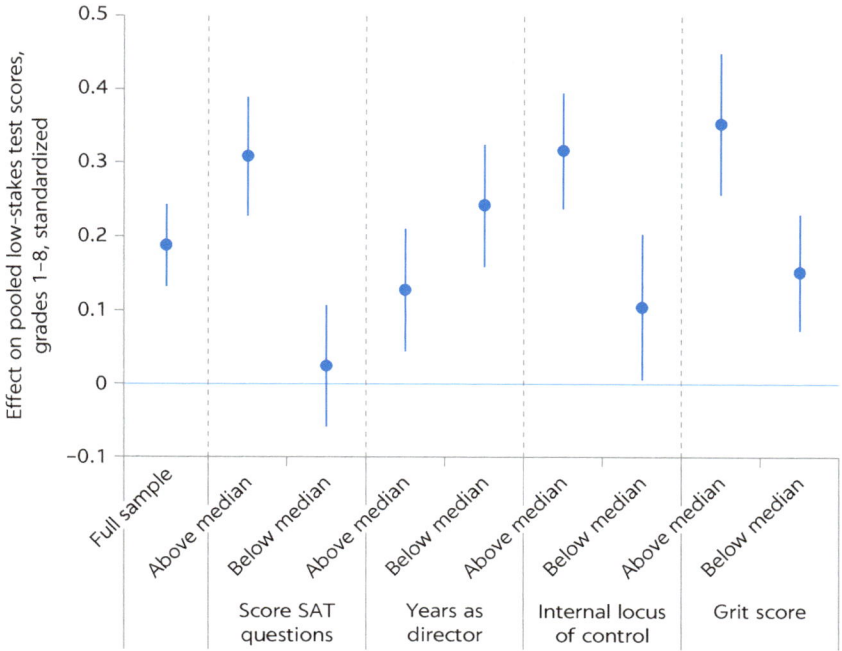

Source: Fryer 2017, table 6C.
Note: This figure shows selected intention-to-treat coefficient and 95 percent confidence interval estimates of the average yearly effects of a management experiment in Houston on student achievement on low-stakes test scores for subgroups of the sample based on director characteristics. Low-stakes tests are the Iowa Test of Basic Skills (ITBS) exams in math, reading, science, and social studies (administered in grades 1–8) and are normalized (across the school district) to have a mean of zero and a standard deviation one for each year, subject, and grade. Similar heterogenous patterns are found for high-stakes tests scores (State of Texas Assessments of Academic Readiness (STAAR) exams in math and reading (administered in grades 3–12)). Number of treated and control schools = 58.

though it ranges from approximately US$1,300 to US$14,600.[6] In comparison, a back-of-the-envelope calculation for the cost of the program evaluated in Fryer (2017) suggests a cost of US$14,655 per school, the upper bound of what is spent on school management training programs in LAC.[7,8] Given these important differences in terms of both design (content and structure) and financial investment, current school management training programs in LAC may not necessarily have a similar impact.

In fact, new evidence is beginning to emerge on the heterogeneous effects of management training programs on students in Latin America. Tavares (2015) uses a fuzzy regression discontinuity design to assess the impacts of a training program for school directors that focused on modern management practices such as developing diagnostics and setting targets for the worst performing schools in Brazil's richest state, São Paulo. She finds that the program improved students' test scores, but only in math and only for lower-performing students (figure 4.4). Tavares presents evidence that the primary channel for these impacts is through changes in management practices, in particular practices related to planning on the basis data, articulating goals, and monitoring progress.

FIGURE 4.4

Results-based schools management training program in São Paulo, Brazil, shows significant positive effects on math scores of low performing students, but not on reading scores

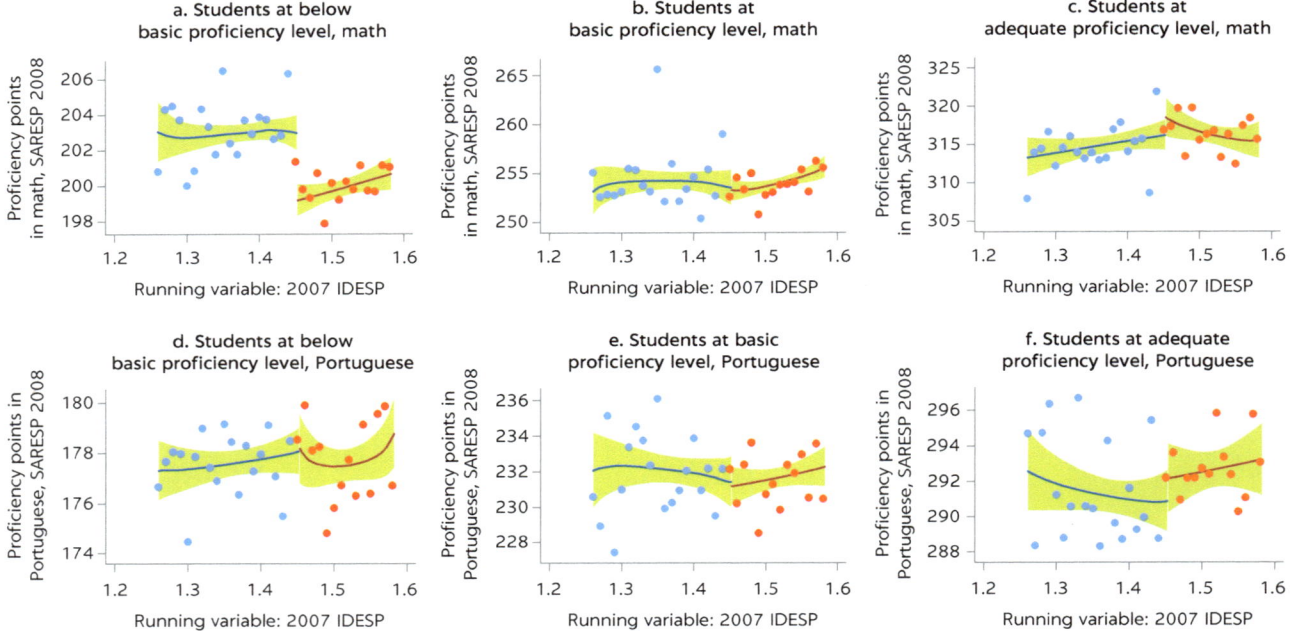

Source: Tavares 2015, figures 3 and 4.
Note: This figure shows the effect of a results-based school management program introduced to the schools with the worst educational outcomes in the state of São Paulo, Brazil. Schools at the bottom 5 percent of the 2007 IDESP distribution of each grade level were selected to be included in the program. Panels plot nonparametric estimations of a fuzzy regression discontinuity design using the 2007 IDESP as the running variable. The blue dots on the left of the running variable represent students in schools where directors were eligible to participate in the management training program while the red dots on the right represent students in schools where directors were not eligible to participate in the program. The program had an impact on math performance of students at below basic proficiency level of approximately 5 points on the proficiency scale—equivalent to approximately 0.14 standard deviations—increasing a typical student's annual learning by 32 percent. Number of schools participating in the program = 379.

For example, schools with directors who completed the training were more proactively monitoring quantitative indicators of student performance and making adjustments in response, which possibly explains why effects on student learning were concentrated among low performers.[9]

In Argentina, De Hoyos, Ganimian, and Holland (2019) provide causal estimates of a training program focused specifically on the use of student learning data for school improvement in the province of La Rioja. The program, which targeted both supervisors (who work across multiple schools) and school directors, as well as teachers, used a much less intensive intervention compared with Fryer (2017).[10] The authors worked with the government to randomly assign 105 public primary schools in La Rioja to one of three groups: (a) a diagnostic feedback group, in which they administered standardized tests in math and reading comprehension at baseline and two follow-ups, and made their results available to the schools through user-friendly reports; (b) a capacity-building group, in which they also conducted professional development workshops and school visits; or (c) a control group, in which they administered the tests only at the second follow-up. This design enables the authors to examine whether disseminating assessment results can be sufficient to prompt improvements in how schools are organized and how classes are taught, or whether dissemination needs to be complemented with support, for example, to distill the results for directors and teachers and to help identify strategies to improve them. These questions are particularly relevant for LAC and for many developing countries in other regions, because data on student learning are starting to be collected more regularly, offering opportunities to dramatically improve the information that managers at all levels (as well as teachers) use.

After two years, the schools using diagnostic feedback outperformed control schools by 0.33 and 0.36 standard deviations in math and reading, respectively (figure 4.5). Consistent with these effects, directors at diagnostic feedback schools were more likely than their control counterparts to report using assessment results in school management (for example, to evaluate teachers, make changes in the curriculum, or inform parents about school quality). Students at these schools were more prone than their control peers to report that their teachers engaged in more instructional activities (for example, copying from the blackboard, explaining topics, and assigning and grading homework). They were also more likely to report positive student-teacher interactions (for example, teachers being nice to them when they ask for help, explaining concepts in multiple ways, and checking that they understand the material).

FIGURE 4.5

Providing school leaders with user-friendly and timely data on student learning raises subsequent test scores, but adding capacity building did not help in La Rioja, Argentina

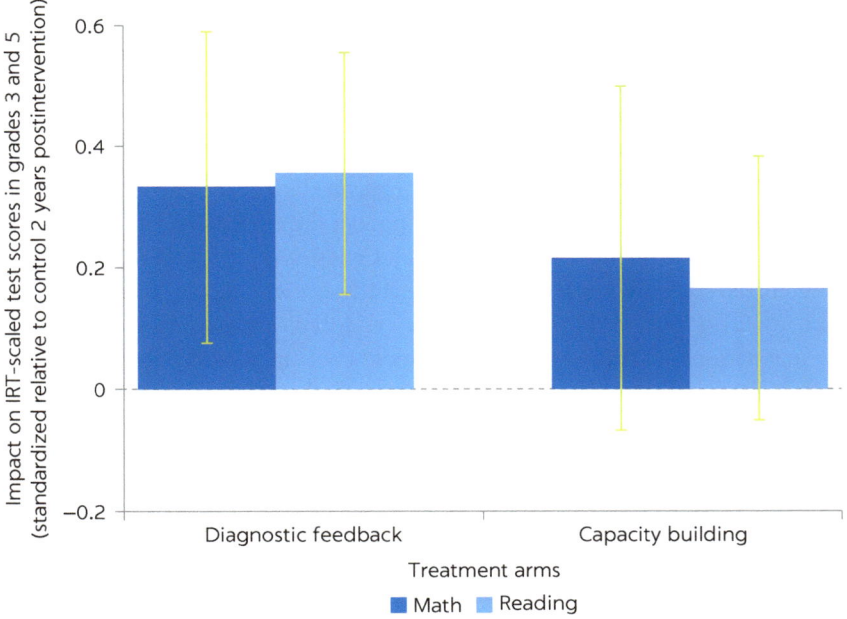

Source: De Hoyos, Ganimian, and Holland 2019, table 3.
Note: This figure shows the intent-to-treat coefficient and 95 percent confidence intervals estimates of the impact on item response theory (IRT)–scaled scores for math and reading for two treatment groups in 2013—diagnostic feedback and capacity building—relative to those of a control group, two years postintervention. Scaled scores were standardized with respect to the control group in 2015 (control mean of 0 and standard deviation of 1). The diagnostic feedback treatment consisted of administering standardized tests at baseline and at two follow-ups and making results available to the schools through user-friendly reports. The capacity-building treatment consisted of providing diagnostic feedback to schools as with the first treatment and also providing schools with professional development workshops for school supervisors, directors, and teachers. Number of treated and control schools = 104; number of students = 10,984.

In spite of being assigned to receive both diagnostic feedback and capacity-building activities, schools' performance in the capacity-building group is not statistically distinguishable from the diagnostic feedback–only group. Three main considerations likely account for this finding. First, by chance, the schools that were randomly assigned to the capacity-building group were already performing considerably below those in the diagnostic feedback group at baseline. Second, capacity-building schools participated in fewer workshops and school visits than expected. Third, each capacity-building activity (that is, workshop or visit) had a positive but limited and statistically insignificant impact on achievement. Consistent with these effects, the authors find less clear evidence of mechanisms that would contribute to effects in capacity-building schools. Directors at these schools were more likely than their control counterparts to report using assessment results to inform school management, but students were no more likely to report changes in instruction. Yet, in nearly all grades and subjects, the authors cannot discard the possibility that diagnostic feedback alone had the same effect as feedback combined with capacity building.

Importantly, the impact of diagnostic feedback demonstrates the potential of large-scale assessments to inform school management and classroom instruction. Upon receiving the assessment results, directors used the feedback as an input for school management decisions, and teachers adjusted their instructional strategies and improved their interactions with students. However, the uneven impact of capacity building illustrates the challenges of implementing meaningful training in developing countries. These results are consistent with those of evaluations of professional development programs across several developing countries, which have also found low take-up and limited effects on learning (see, for example, Angrist and Lavy 2001; Yoshikawa and others 2015; Zhang and others 2010).

In Guatemala, Haimovich, Vazquez, and Adelman (forthcoming) assess the impacts of a different type of training program, one that supports primary school directors exclusively to reduce school dropout in the transition from primary to lower secondary school. The program's pilot phase was designed as a four-arm randomized controlled trial across 4,000 public primary schools—one treatment that provides knowledge to school directors and sixth-grade teachers about simple and actionable measures to help students stay in school, through a user-friendly guidance manual and half-day training (the *how*); a second treatment that adds information about which students are most at risk of dropping out (the *who*); a third treatment that adds small behavioral nudges to encourage school directors to prioritize dropout as a problem to be addressed; and the control group. Compared to the control group of schools, and controlling for student-level characteristics and school-fixed effects, assignment to the program (pooling across the three treatment groups) significantly reduces dropout by 1.3 percentage points (about 4 percent of the baseline dropout rate). When taking noncompliance into consideration, Haimovich, Vazquez, and Adelman (forthcoming) estimate a dropout reduction of 3.1 percentage points among treated students. The effect of the program is statistically indistinguishable across the three treatments arms, suggesting that the basic intervention on *how* dropout can be prevented is mostly driving the impact. These results point to the potential that focused training programs for school directors may hold for addressing not only student learning but also other important student outcomes such as dropout. At the same time, the authors observe important variation across subgroups, which suggests that this type of capacity-building approach is only effective when other

FIGURE 4.6

Focused support program for directors to keep children in school helps reduce dropouts in Guatemala, particularly for larger schools and for boys

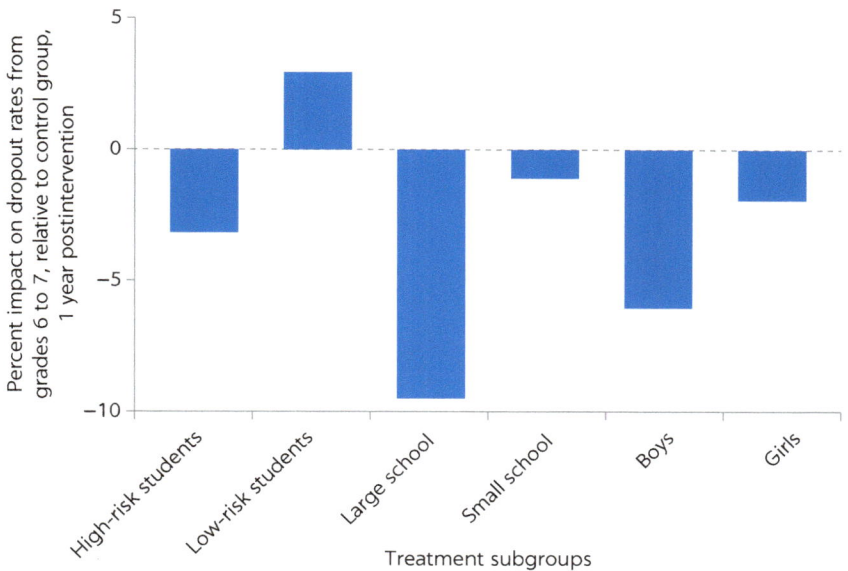

Source: Haimovich, Vazquez, and Adelman, forthcoming.
Note: This figure shows the intent-to-treat impact of three variations of a government training program across subgroups of students (the overall impact is statistically indistinguishable across the three variations). The variations are (a) providing knowledge to school directors and sixth-grade teachers about simple, actionable measures to help students stay in school, through a user-friendly guidance manual and half-day training; (b) adding information about which students are most at risk of dropping out; and (c) adding small behavioral nudges to encourage school directors to prioritize dropout as a problem to be addressed. High- and low-risk students are defined by the probability of dropout estimated in the early warning system. Large and small schools are defined as being above and below the median number of students in the school. Boys and girls are defined through reported gender in administrative data. Number of treated and control schools: 4,400; number of students: 145,628.

constraints are not binding (figure 4.6). For example, dropout reductions are concentrated among large primary schools, which are more likely to be located near a secondary school, and among boys, who may face fewer pressures from their households than girls to take on domestic labor or enter into early marriage.

Several other impact evaluations are under way across the LAC region and other parts of the world, which will advance researchers' knowledge about whether and how management training programs for current directors can change practices and ultimately student outcomes. For example, Romero and others (2021) have recently presented results for a large-scale, results-driven managerial capacity training for school directors across seven states in Mexico. In this evaluation, nearly 1,500 directors were randomly assigned to management training programs or a control group, and outcomes were tracked through the collection of D-WMS management data as well as administrative data on student outcomes, including dropout rates and standardized test scores. The training programs across the seven states vary in intensity (ranging from several weeks to one year of training) and in the range of topics covered, but all include three elements: (a) the use of a classroom observation method, (b) the use of two diagnostic tools to assess students' math and Spanish proficiency levels and provide feedback to the teachers, and (c) improved leadership and use of results-based managerial practices. The authors, however, find no impact of management training on student test scores, even when the management training intervention was combined with cash grants.

Although the literature on training is limited, there are almost no well-identified studies on the impacts of performance incentives for directors or system managers on management quality or student outcomes.[11] For teachers, systematic reviews of educational interventions in developing countries find that financial incentives for increasing student performance are cost-effective when they work. However, the impacts vary greatly depending on the context and details of the incentive scheme, and they can sometimes elicit dysfunctional responses, such as focusing teaching exclusively on test preparation or cheating (Evans and Popova 2016; Ganimian and Murnane 2016; McEwan 2015).

In addition, performance pay schemes can have screening effects beyond their direct incentive effects, attracting different types of people to positions that offer performance pay. Observational evidence from the United States suggests that districts that introduce pay-for-performance schemes for teachers see a subsequent increase in the quality of their applicant pools (Jones and Hartney 2017; Neal 2011). Different types of incentive schemes—rewarding inputs financially or providing nonfinancial rewards for results, such as giving priority in choosing postings—have been studied even less in education and across different sectors (Finan, Olken, and Pande 2015). Given the multifaceted nature of school directors and other managerial roles, and the correlational results of Rasul and Rogger (2018) and Rasul, Rogger, and Williams (forthcoming) discussed in previous chapters, effective incentive schemes for education managers may be even more challenging to develop than for teachers and should be considered carefully.[12]

ALIGNING LAYERS OF THE SYSTEM

Beyond the individual skills and characteristics of school-level managers, the quality of management depends on how well-functioning the education system is above the school level. As described in previous chapters, public school directors across LAC have relatively limited autonomy over many key decision areas, and local, regional, and national education bureaucrats may have important influence over the quality of education service delivery and ultimately student outcomes. One of the few well-identified studies on this topic comes from Lavy and Boiko (2017), who exploit a quasi-random assignment of superintendents to schools in Israel to estimate superintendent value added. In the Israeli system, superintendents are the CEOs of a cluster of schools within a school district or a local school authority, and their many responsibilities include directly managing their schools' directors. They find that a 1 standard deviation increase in superintendents' management quality increases students' test scores by 0.04 standard deviations, a small but significant effect, particularly given that each superintendent is responsible for several hundred students (Lavy and Boiko 2017).

Yet in many middle- and low-income countries, bureaucrats above the school level appear to focus on transmitting documents and ensuring rule compliance, rather than what matters most for student outcomes. Mbiti (2016) describes, for example, how in Tanzania only 30 percent of directors report that the most recent visit of their local inspector focused on teaching or learning, suggesting that strengthening the capacities of such higher level managers could be an effective lever for improving student outcomes.

The alignment and cooperation of bureaucrats at different levels are also likely to matter for how schools perform, but the few rigorous evaluations conducted on programs focused on these aspects have had mixed results to date.[13] One randomized evaluation of a program in Madagascar aimed at strengthening basic processes related to teaching and learning at each step of the service delivery chain, through tools, data, and training. That study finds that the management practices of system actors, including school directors, improved, and that student attendance increased and grade repetition fell (Lassibille and others 2010; Lassibille 2016). However, a program with a similar theory of change, implemented in the Indian state of Madhya Pradesh, was found to have no impacts on school functioning or on student learning because of poor implementation and bureaucrats' strong existing incentives to focus on paperwork and appearing to be busy (Muralidharan and Singh 2020).

In LAC, Paes de Barros and others (2018) contribute to this literature by evaluating a decade-long program—Jovem de Futuro (JdeF)—in Brazil that aims to both build management capacity and align local actors—directors, supervisors, and regional directors—around common, student-centered objectives. To provide training and ongoing support for implementing a classic management method of plan-do-check-act (PDCA), the program leverages Brazil's well-developed national system of education quality indicators. To promote strong vertical coordination with actors at all levels of the education system, the program taps into existing organizational structures, focuses more on aligning processes than on content, and conducts impact evaluations on all waves of implementation to inform continuous improvement.

The third and current iteration of the program consists of multiple complementary components. The main component is a results-focused management training program consisting of 68 classroom hours for department technicians, regional leaders, and supervisors, as well as 48 classroom hours and 120 distance hours for school directors and pedagogical coordinators. As part of this training and ongoing support, the program equips managers with goals, protocols, and management practices that facilitate, stimulate, and promote expertise in the PDCA cycle: (a) participatory planning, geared toward achieving student achievement results (goals) and strongly based on evidence (*plan*); (b) monitoring of the plan's implementation (*do*); (c) assessment and analysis of the results obtained (*check*); and (d) identification of adjustments, necessary route changes, and redesign of actions (*act*). Two features that are particularly novel about JdeF is the emphasis placed on the role of the local supervisor, as an actor who both supports and monitors school directors' implementation of the PDCA cycle, and the establishment of "formal management circuits" through which school directors, supervisors, and higher-level regional officials regularly meet to discuss progress against their goals and exchange advice.

Randomized rollout of each iteration of the program across public high schools in different states based on matched groups enables Paes de Barros and others (2018) to estimate the causal impact of JdeF on student achievement in math and Portuguese. After three years of program participation (a full cycle of secondary school), students in treated schools had Portuguese and math test scores 4.4 and 4.8 points (0.09 and 0.12 standard deviations), respectively, higher than students in control schools (figure 4.7). The authors assess the

FIGURE 4.7
Management capacity building program focused on aligning local actors to improve student achievement has had positive results across Brazil

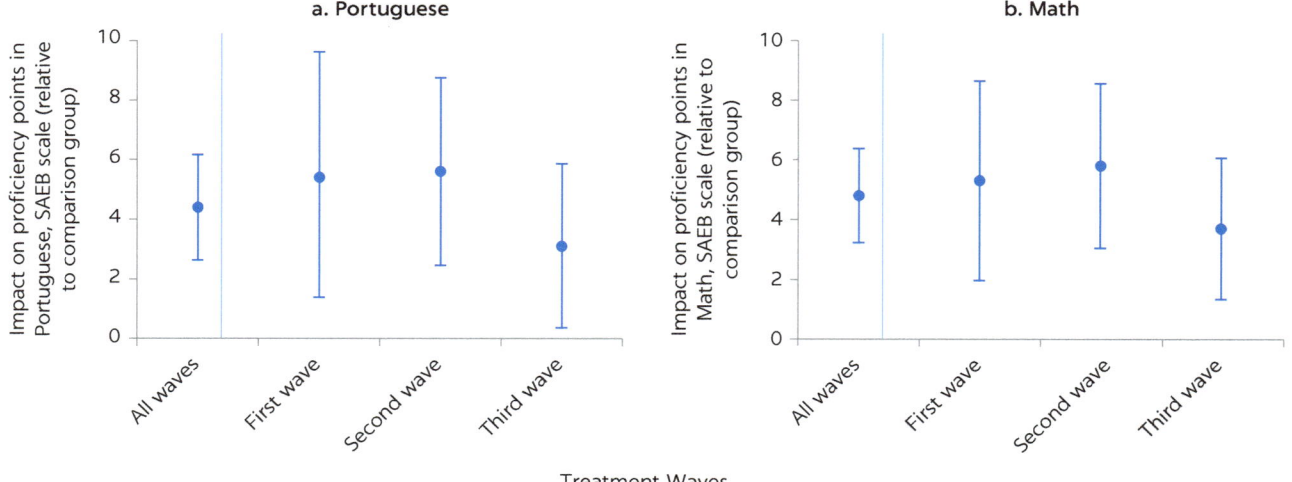

Source: Paes de Barros and others 2018.
Note: This figure shows the intention-to-treat coefficient and 95% confidence interval estimates in Portuguese and math scores after three years of participation in the Jovem de Futuro program (table 10). The program was implemented across three waves: the first wave (2008–13) corresponds to schools in the states of Belo Horizonte, São Paulo, and Rio de Janeiro; the second wave (2012–15) corresponds to schools in Ceará, Goiás, Mato Grosso do Sul, and Pará; and the third wave (2015–18) corresponds to schools in Espírito Santo, Pará, and Piauí. Standard deviations in Portuguese and math scores in public high schools are 48 and 40 points, respectively. Number of participating schools = 1,732.

relative magnitude of these impacts in various ways, and find that JdeF costs about 5 percent of public expenditures per student for secondary school, while it increases the amount that students learn on average during secondary school by about 30 percent. Interestingly, the impacts of the program across all three iterations are not statistically distinguishable from each other. This suggests that the focus of the third iteration on system alignment was relatively powerful, as the first two iterations included substantial additional financing for treatment schools (US$100 per student per year), which was dropped from the program by the third iteration.

NOTES

1. Directors of schools participating in TERCE self-reported being selected by the community: 40 percent of directors in Paraguay, 22 percent in Panama, and 16 percent in Guatemala. In all other TERCE-participating countries the responses are below 10 percent.
2. For theoretical framing and empirical evidence from other public sectors, see Besley and Coate (2003) and Whalley (2013).
3. They first develop an extension of the teacher-value-added model to measure director effectiveness in an attempt to disentangle the effect of directors from other school-related factors. Using Chilean administrative data and student-level grades, they find that a 1 standard deviation increase in their measure of director effectiveness is associated with an increase in student grades by 0.22 standard deviations.
4. For example, in the Dominican Republic, local, district, and regional directors of the public education system were selected through merit-based competition for the first time in 2017, as part of the country's broader efforts to strengthen decentralized system management.

5. Results presented in figure 4.3 are for low-stakes exams. A similar pattern holds for high-stakes exams, as described in detail in Fryer 2017.
6. Only 8 out of 13 programs provided information on cost per capita. Reported costs were adjusted using a purchasing parity conversion factor for 2014, which is equivalent to the cost provided in Fryer 2017, appendix C.
7. Fryer (2017, appendix C) reports that there were 24,000 students and 31,000 students in treatment and control schools each year, respectively, and calculates that the cost per student in treatment schools per year is US$9.61 and the cost per student in control schools is US$0.35. That is, approximately 4.5 percent of the costs per year were directed to control schools and 95.5 percent were directed to treatment schools. Thus, out of the US$445,000 spent over the two years, approximately US$425,000 was spent with the 29 treatment schools (this includes the cost of materials used in training, the technology systems used to manage student data, the salary of the chief management officer, and the cost of preparing interim assessments). This results in a cost of US$14,655 per school.
8. Although directors were required to participate in the training program, directors were encouraged to invite other members of their leadership teams, including assistant principals, deans of curriculum and instruction, deans of students, and other instructional leaders.
9. Also, the training program occurred in a broader context of accountability in Brazil, where school staff bonuses are based on publicly disclosed performance indicators, which may have been conducive to behavior change among the program's participants.
10. See De Hoyos, Garcia-Moreno, and Patrinos (2017) for the positive results of an intervention providing data on student learning and technical assistance to design school improvement plans in Mexico, as well as a review of related literature.
11. One of the few exceptions is McEwan and Santibañez (2005), which draws on the structure of incentives in Mexico's Carrera Magisterial to estimate the effects of salary incentives for student learning on school directors. They find no effect.
12. Research from the United States under the No Child Left Behind legislation suggests that focusing on limited indicators and encouraging strong public pressure for accountability can indeed end up targeting the wrong directors for dismissal and having negative impacts on student outcomes (Cullen and others 2016).
13. As described in detail in chapter 2, Adelman and others (forthcoming) find that a measure of coherence across system actors in their understanding of roles is positively correlated with student learning.

REFERENCES

Adelman, Melissa, Renata Lemos, Reema Nayar, and Maria Jose Vargas. Forthcoming. "(In)coherence in the Management of Education Systems in Latin America." Working paper, World Bank, Washington, DC.

Akhtari, Mitra, Diana Moreira, and Laura Trucco. Forthcoming. "Political Turnover, Bureaucratic Turnover, and the Quality of Public Services." *American Economic Review*.

Andrews, Matt, Lant Pritchett, and Michael Woolcock. 2017. *Building State Capability: Evidence, Analysis, Action*. New York: Oxford University Press.

Angrist, Joshua, and Victor Lavy. 2001. "Does Teacher Training Affect Pupil Learning? Evidence from Matched Comparisons in Jerusalem Public Schools." *Journal of Labor Economics* 19 (2): 343–69.

Ashraf, Nava, Oriana Bandiera, Edward Davenport, and Scott Lee. 2020. "Losing Prosociality in the Quest for Talent? Sorting, Selection, and Productivity in the Delivery of Public Services." *American Economic Review* 110 (5): 1355–94.

Barber, Michael, Fenton Whelan, and Michael Clark. 2010. "Capturing the Leadership Premium: How the World's Top School Systems Are Building Leadership Capacity for the Future." McKinsey & Company. https://www.mckinsey.com/industries/public-and-social-sector/our-insights/capturing-the-leadership-premium.

Besley, Timothy, and Stephen Coate. 2003. "Elected Versus Appointed Regulators: Theory and Evidence." *Journal of the European Economic Association* 1 (5): 1176–1206.

Bruns, Barbara, and Javier Luque. 2015. *Great Teachers. How to Raise Student Learning in Latin America and the Caribbean.* Washington, DC: World Bank.

Corcoran, Sean, Amy Schwartz, and Meryle Weinstein. 2012 "Training Your Own: The Impact of New York City's Aspiring Principals Program on Student Achievement." *Educational Evaluation and Policy Analysis* 34 (2): 232–53.

Cullen, Julie Berry, Eric A. Hanushek, Gregory Phelan, and Steven G. Rivkin. 2016. "Performance Information and Personnel Decisions in the Public Sector: The Case of School Principals." NBER Working Paper 22881, National Bureau of Economic Research, Cambridge, MA.

Dal Bó, Ernesto, Frederico Finan, and Martín Rossi. 2013. "Strengthening State Capabilities: The Role of Financial Incentives in the Call to Public Service." *Quarterly Journal of Economics* 128 (3):1169–218.

De Hoyos, Rafael, Alejandro Ganimian, and Peter Holland. 2019. "Teaching *with* the Test: Experimental Evidence on Diagnostic Feedback and Capacity-Building for Public Schools in Argentina." *World Bank Economic Review.* lhz026, https://doi.org/10.1093/wber/lhz026.

De Hoyos, Rafael, Vicente Garcia-Moreno, and Harry Patrinos. 2017. "The Impact of an Accountability Intervention with Diagnostic Feedback: Evidence from Mexico." *Economics of Education Review* 58: 123–40.

de Ree, Joppe, Karthik Muralidharan, Menno Pradhan, and Halsey Rogers. 2018. "Double for Nothing? Experimental Evidence on an Unconditional Teacher Salary Increase in Indonesia." *Quarterly Journal of Economics* 133 (2): 993–1039.

Evans, David, and Anna Popova. 2016. "What Really Works to Improve Learning in Developing Countries? An Analysis of Divergent Findings in Systematic Reviews." *World Bank Research Observer* 31 (2): 242–70.

Finan, Frederico, Benjamin Olken, and Rohini Pande. 2015. "The Personnel Economics of the State." NBER Working Paper 21825, National Bureau of Economic Research, Cambridge, MA.

Fryer, Roland G. Jr. 2017. "Management and Student Achievement: Evidence from a Randomized Field Experiment." NBER Working Paper 23437, National Bureau of Economic Research, Cambridge, MA.

Ganimian, Alejandro, and Richard Murnane. 2016. "Improving Educational Outcomes in Developing Countries: Lessons from Rigorous Evaluations." *Review of Educational Research* 86 (3): 719–55.

Haimovich, Francisco, Emmanuel Vazquez, and Melissa Adelman. Forthcoming. "Scalable Early Warning Systems for School Dropout Prevention: Evidence from a 4,000-School Randomized Control Trial." Working paper, World Bank, Washington, DC.

Jensen, Ben, Phoebe Downing, and Anna Clark. 2017. "Preparing to Lead: Lessons in Principal Development from High-Performing Education Systems." Washington, DC: National Center on Education and the Economy.

Jones, Michael, and Michael Hartney. 2017. "Show Who the Money? Teacher Sorting Patterns and Performance Pay across U.S. School Districts." *Public Administration Review* 77 (6): 919–31.

Lassibille, Gerard. 2016. "Improving the Management Style of School Principals: Results from a Randomized Trial." *Education Economics* 24(2): 121-141.

Lassibille, Gerard, Jee-Peng Tan, Cornelia Jesse, and Trang Van Nguyen. 2010. "Managing for Results in Primary Education in Madagascar: Evaluating the Impact of Selected Workflow Interventions." *World Bank Economic Review* 24 (2): 303–29.

Lavy, Victor, and Adi Boiko. 2017. "Management Quality in Public Education: Superintendent Value-Added, Student Outcomes and Mechanisms." NBER Working Paper 24028, National Bureau of Economic Research, Cambridge, MA.

Lemos, Renata, and Caio Piza. Forthcoming. "Manager Selection and Student Learning: Evidence from Peru." Working paper, World Bank, Washington, DC.

Mbiti, Isaac. 2016. "The Need for Accountability in Education in Developing Countries." *Journal of Economic Perspectives* 30 (3): 109–32.

McEwan, Patrick. 2015. "Improving Learning in Primary Schools of Developing Countries: A Meta-Analysis of Randomized Experiments." *Review of Educational Research* 85 (3): 353–94.

McEwan, Patrick, and Lucrecia Santibáñez. 2005. "Teacher and Principal Incentives in Mexico." In *Incentives to Improve Teaching, Lessons from Latin America*, edited by Emiliana Vegas. Washington, DC: World Bank.

Muñoz, Pablo, and Mounu Prem. 2020. "Managers' Productivity and Labor Market: Evidence from School Principals." Working papers 40, Red Investigadores de Economía.

Muralidharan, Karthik, and Abhijeet Singh. 2020. "Improving Public Sector Management at Scale? Experimental Evidence on School Governance in India." NBER Working Paper 28129, National Bureau of Economic Research, Cambridge, MA.

Neal, Derek. 2011. "The Design of Performance Pay in Education." In *Handbook of the Economics of Education*, edited by E. A. Hanushek, S. Machin, and L. Woessmann (vol. 4), 495–550. North Holland, Amsterdam.

Paes de Barros, Ricardo, Mirela de Carvalho, Samuel Franco, Beatriz Franco, Ricardo Henriques, and Laura Machado. 2018. "Assessment of the Impact of the Jovem de Futuro Program on Learning." Working paper. http://documents1.worldbank.org/curated/es/825101561723584640/pdf/Assessment-of-the-Impact-of-the-Jovem-de-Futuro-Program-on-Learning.pdf.

Pereda, Paula, Andrea Lucchesi, Karen Mendes, and Antonio Bresolin. 2020. "Evaluating the Impact of the Selection Process of Principals in Brazilian Public Schools." *Nova Economia* 29 (2): 591–621.

Pritchett, Lant, and Michael Woolcock. 2004. "Solutions When the Solution Is the Problem: Arraying the Disarray in Development." World Development 32 (2): 191–212.

Rasul, Imran, and Daniel Rogger. 2018. "Management of Bureaucrats and Public Service Delivery: Evidence from the Nigerian Civil Service." *The Economic Journal* 128 (608): 413–46.

Rasul, Imran, Daniel Rogger, and Martin Williams. Forthcoming. "Management, Organizational Performance, and Task Clarity: Evidence from Ghana's Civil Service." *Journal of Public Administration Research and Theory*.

Romero, Mauricio, Juan Bedoya, Monica Yanez-Pagans, Marcela Silveyra, and Rafael de Hoyos. 2021. "School Management, Grants, and Test Scores." Policy Research Working Paper 9535, World Bank, Washington, DC.

Tavares, Priscilla. 2015. "The Impact of School Management Practices on Educational Performance: Evidence from Public Schools in São Paulo." *Economics of Education Review* 48: 1–15.

Whalley, Alexander. 2013. "Elected Versus Appointed Policy Makers: Evidence from City Treasurers." *Journal of Law & Economics* 56 (1): 39–81.

Yoshikawa, Hirokazu, Diana Leyva, Catherine E. Snow, Ernesto Treviño, M. Clara Barata, Christina Weiland, Celia J. Gomez, Lorenzo Moreno, Andrea Rolla, Nikhit D'Sa, and Mary Catherine Arbour. 2015. "Experimental Impacts of a Teacher Professional Development Program in Chile on Preschool Classroom Quality and Child Outcomes." *Developmental Psychology* 51 (3): 309–22.

Zhang, Meilan, Mary Lundeberg, Matthew J. Koehler, and Jan Eberhardt. 2010. "Understanding Affordances and Challenges of Three Types of Video for Teacher Professional Development." *Teaching and Teacher Education* 27 (2): 454–62.

5 Taking Stock and Looking Ahead

A POLICY AND RESEARCH AGENDA

How can countries make sustainable gains in student learning at scale? This is a pressing question for Latin America and the Caribbean (LAC)—and the developing world more broadly—as countries seek to build human capital to drive sustainable growth. Significant progress in access has expanded coverage such that nearly all children in the region attend primary school, but many do not gain basic skills and drop out before completing secondary school, in part because of low-quality service delivery. The easily measurable inputs are well known, and the end goal is relatively clear, but raising student achievement at scale remains a challenge. Why?

In this study, we have proposed that part of the answer lies in management—the practices, managers, and organizational structures that guide how inputs into the education system are translated into outputs, and ultimately outcomes. Individual interventions can succeed in the short run, but virtually any initiative or program, from coaching classroom teachers to providing school meals, requires effective management from public education systems, in addition to adequate financing, to reach the majority of children in LAC. Evidence from across countries participating in the Program for International Student Assessment (PISA) supports this idea: moving from the bottom to the top quartile of school management quality is associated with approximately an additional three months of schooling (Leaver, Lemos, and Scur 2019).

HOW TO MEASURE MANAGEMENT AS A CATALYST FOR IMPROVEMENT

We define management as practices employed with the objective of coordinating resources to achieve a common goal—such as allocating tasks and monitoring their completion, setting the pace of work, and administering both human and physical resources. These practices help determine how critical inputs into the student learning process—from teachers to textbooks to infrastructure—come together in schools and classrooms. The proximate determinants of these practices include the managers and organizational structures in place at all levels of education systems, which in turn are shaped by the political, socioeconomic, and broader characteristics of any given context.

To organize and simplify the broad concept of management in public education, we consider three main levels: management of individual schools, management of the middle layers (defined units such as a local administrative district or a central technical unit), and management of an education system as a whole (such as a basic education ministry).

Several new instruments now exist to measure management at every level, including instruments developed as part of research for this study. These tools measure the supply and quality of key practices for managing day-to-day school activities and dealing with shocks, as well as the quality of management above the school level in the education system (described in detail in chapter 2). Moreover, thanks in part to growing participation in international standardized assessments like the Regional and Comparative Explanatory Study (ERCE) and PISA, and also to new measurement instruments, the availability of data on managers themselves and the organizational structures around them is also increasing.

The data from these different sources can inform policy makers in several ways. They can provide snapshots of how well schools or systems are run to inform policy at the macro level; they can identify specific areas where practices can be strengthened to inform programs and intervention areas; they can track the impacts of changes in policies or programs on the practices of managers in the system; and they can be used to inform managers about their own performance, providing feedback and opportunities for improvement. Continued research to develop informative measurement instruments, including questions that can be used in large-scale questionnaires, will be key to advancing our understanding of management and managers across education systems.

HOW MANAGEMENT MATTERS FOR EDUCATION OUTCOMES

In chapter 3, we describe *how* management matters in education, with new theoretical and empirical contributions to the literature. At the school level, we describe how stronger management practices can affect the selection and incentives of teachers and students, and how stronger operations management practices are correlated with higher teacher motivation, teacher effort, and student attention in LAC's public education systems, where people management is relatively weak (Leaver, Lemos, and Scur 2019). This theoretical framework helps to organize a small but broad and growing global literature that examines the relationships between management practices, teachers, and student outcomes. We also use data from Haiti's experience with Hurricane Matthew to present new empirical evidence showing that schools with stronger management practices not only are better able to cope with shocks but also adopt more effective disaster risk management practices in the aftermath of a shock (Adelman, Baron, and Lemos, forthcoming).

These contributions only begin to get inside the black box of how management at the school level affects student outcomes. A future research agenda would address additional questions, including (a) how management practices differ in the low-cost private school sector that has been rapidly growing in many countries; (b) how management affects families' decisions over which schools to select for their students, and families' decisions over how much to participate in school management themselves; and (c) whether specific management practices are most important to achieving specific student outcomes (and how these relationships interact with features of the context). In addition, much remains to be learned about effective management approaches for small (often rural) schools and other schools that lack an official director.

At the middle layers of education systems, such as local administrative districts, central technical units, and autonomous institutes, quantitative research on how management matters is scarce. Innovations in measuring management in a consistent way across different government structures represents an important area for future research, including Rasul and Rogger's adaptation of the World Management Survey (WMS) instrument for public agencies, coupled with better measures of these layers' outputs and performance.

At the system level, we contribute to the broader literature on institutions in education, with new empirical evidence on the organizational structure of public basic education systems (Adelman and others, forthcoming). The authors develop new measures of the completeness, coherence, and quality of the functioning of these systems in Brazil, the Dominican Republic, Guatemala, and Peru. Several key findings emerge from this approach. First, the allocation of core system tasks is incomplete (not clearly assigned in regulation). Large percentages of sampled bureaucrats across countries do not share a common understanding of the allocation of core tasks (incoherence), either compared with legislation or with each other, and measures of the quality of system functioning (or upstream service delivery) are particularly low for personnel management. The authors also find suggestive evidence that coherence between bureaucrats' understanding of the allocation of tasks matters for the outcomes produced by public education systems. Coherence between a school director, her local education official, and regulation is positively correlated with student learning outcomes, suggesting that coherence matters for how education systems function and ultimately for student outcomes.

These results demonstrate that the management of public education systems can be measured in an increasingly consistent and meaningful way across countries. Future research could build on the ESCS developed by Adelman and others (forthcoming)—including addressing the shortcomings discussed in chapter 3—to expand this work to other countries and continue to deepen our understanding of how systems matter for educational achievement.

HOW TO IMPROVE MANAGEMENT: SELECTING, SUPPORTING, AND ALIGNING

Descriptive research coupled with a growing number of rigorous evaluations identify three main approaches to strengthening management in schools and systems: improving selection processes for managers; creating or improving management career frameworks with training, support, and incentives; and aligning system actors toward delivering quality services. Chapter 4 describes the latest research on each of these approaches in turn, highlighting several promising opportunities for policy makers seeking to strengthen management in their education systems.

In countries across LAC and the world, many public sector managers, including school directors, are politically appointed without binding merit-based criteria, or they earn their position solely by virtue of being the longest-serving teacher or other staff member. These processes are not likely to reliably select for the skills and motivation needed to effectively drive improvements in student outcomes. High-performing education systems globally take a purposeful approach to the development and selection of managerial staff. Though these processes cannot be easily transplanted across contexts (for a myriad of reasons described in chapter 4), moving toward more rigorous selection methods holds promise as a way to improve the quality of managers coming into the system. New research on the experiences of several recent policy changes in director selection methods in Brazil, Chile, and Peru show that moving away from non-merit-based appointments can change who is selected to lead schools and their subsequent performance, but the quality of the candidate pool, local conditions, and broader political economy considerations are critical to the ultimate impacts of these reforms on student outcomes (Pereda and others 2020, Muñoz and Prem 2020, Lemos and Piza forthcoming).

In terms of supporting managers throughout their careers, emerging evidence suggests that practical preservice, induction, and in-service training programs that focus on specific practices tied to improving student outcomes can have sizable impacts on managerial practices and ultimately student outcomes. In Argentina, providing school leaders with easy-to-understand learning data for their students and guidance on how to use it raised subsequent student test scores by about 0.3 standard deviations (De Hoyos, Ganimian, and Holland 2019). In Guatemala, providing school leaders with actionable information on supporting students to help them stay in school reduced dropout by 4 percent (Haimovich, Vazquez, and Adelman, forthcoming). However, as described in chapter 2, several government-supported in-service training programs in the region take a much broader approach, covering a wide range of management topics with a limited emphasis on practice, and consequently may have much smaller impacts on managerial practices and student outcomes, if any.

In many LAC countries, and the world, the quality of services provided by public schools depends as much on the bureaucrats who sit above the school level as it does on school directors themselves. As described in Bloom and others (2015), about half of the variance in school management practices globally is at the country level, more than any other sector they had studied thus far. In Brazil, a management capacity-building program that aligns school directors and local education managers around specific student outcome targets increased student test scores by about 0.1 standard deviations and was highly cost-effective (Paes de Barros and others 2018). Such management initiatives, that articulate clear goals for student outcomes and align system actors around these goals based on a shared understanding of each actor's responsibilities, hold promise for many LAC countries that have already advanced in measuring student outcomes.

Taken together, this body of work suggests that policy makers can do much to strengthen management in their systems. Some reforms are largely technical and can work within existing structures. For example, clarifying allocation of responsibilities and articulating common objectives at each level of the system, or building school directors' capacity to provide effective (but essentially nonbinding) feedback to teachers, can have positive, cost-effective impacts with relatively modest investments. Other reforms, such as reallocating roles and responsibilities within a ministry to improve coherence or revising selection mechanisms for managers, are likely to disturb entrenched interests and require significant political will to enact. Some reforms, such as developing and implementing new comprehensive training programs, require a real commitment of financial and technical resources.

AN AGENDA FOR FUTURE RESEARCH

At the same time, an exciting research agenda lies ahead, as school systems test and refine approaches to more effectively select and support their managers and to align different units and levels of the system toward learning. Regarding selection, much remains to be understood about how to attract and select individuals who will make the best managers at schools or at higher levels in developing countries. Success in high-income countries with approaches that rely heavily on high-quality candidate pools and the judgment of system actors may not be immediately applicable in many developing countries. However, recent experiences in several LAC countries with shifts toward competitive exams, direct election by communities, or other mechanisms suggest a multitude of alternative approaches that could substantially change the composition of who becomes a manager. Further research on these and other changes would contribute greatly to the understanding of how to improve management in education, and to the broader body of knowledge on how to improve the quality of public sector workers.

A small number of studies have shown that training and support can make managers better, but much more research is needed to understand (a) what features of in-service training matter, building on data collected with the newly developed School Management Training Survey Instrument; (b) what features of the broader context matter, for example, in terms of the allocation of responsibilities; (c) the channels through which in-service director training can affect student outcomes (through directors' reallocation of time or improvement in the quality of their work, for example); and (d) whether training for higher-level managers can also be effective. In addition, little evidence exists on these same questions for preservice training or induction, representing another rich research agenda. Finally, on system alignment, quantitative research is quite scarce and represents an important area for future study. Initiatives to strengthen system alignment can take many forms, from a narrow but deep focus on a specific function (and how well it is carried out from national policy through to service delivery at schools), to a wide but thin focus on how policies align with each other at the national level. We have little evidence so far on any of these types of initiatives but will need that evidence to support countries in making improvements at scale.

As countries seek to tackle the student learning crisis in LAC and around the world, strengthening management should be central to their approach in order to achieve results that can be sustained at scale. Given the urgency of the learning crisis, which is only being exacerbated by the COVID-19 pandemic, efforts to strengthen management will need to advance alongside research. Careful design of policy and program changes, coupled with rigorous assessment whenever feasible, would therefore serve both to inform countries' own decision-making and to build our broader understanding of what works well, what does not work and why, to strengthen management at different levels of public education systems.

REFERENCES

Adelman, Melissa, Juan Baron, and Renata Lemos. Forthcoming. "Managing Shocks in Education: Evidence from Hurricane Matthew in Haiti." Working paper, World Bank, Washington, DC.

Adelman, Melissa, Renata Lemos, Reema Nayar, and Maria Jose Vargas. Forthcoming. "(In)coherence in the Management of Education Systems in Latin America." Working paper, World Bank, Washington, DC.

Bloom, Nicholas, Renata Lemos, Raffaella Sadun, and John Van Reenen. 2015. "Does Management Matter in Schools?" *The Economic Journal* 125 (584): 647–74.

De Hoyos, Rafael, Alejandro Ganimian, and Peter Holland. 2019. "Teaching with the Test: Experimental Evidence on Diagnostic Feedback and Capacity-Building for Public Schools in Argentina." *World Bank Economic Review.* lhz026, https://doi.org/10.1093/wber/lhz026.

Haimovich, Francisco, Emmanuel Vazquez, and Melissa Adelman. Forthcoming. "Scalable Early Warning Systems for School Dropout Prevention: Evidence from a 4,000-School Randomized Control Trial." Working paper, World Bank, Washington, DC.

Leaver, Clare, Renata Lemos, and Daniela Scur. 2019. "Measuring and Explaining Management in Schools: New Approaches Using Public Data." Policy Research Working Paper 9053, World Bank, Washington, DC.

Lemos, Renata, and Caio Piza. Forthcoming. "Manager Selection and Student Learning: Evidence from Peru." Working paper, World Bank, Washington, DC.

Muñoz, Pablo, and Mounu Prem. 2020. "Managers' Productivity and Labor Market: Evidence from School Principals." Working papers 40, Red Investigadores de Economía.

Paes de Barros, Ricardo, Mirela de Carvalho, Samuel Franco, Beatriz Franco, Ricardo Henriques, and Laura Machado. 2018. "Assessment of the Impact of the Jovem de Futuro Program on Learning." Working paper. http://documents1.worldbank.org/curated/es/825101561723584640/pdf/Assessment-of-the-Impact-of-the-Jovem-de-Futuro-Program-on-Learning.pdf.

Pereda, Paula, Andrea Lucchesi, Karen Mendes, and Antonio Bresolin. 2020. "Evaluating the Impact of the Selection Process of Principals in Brazilian Public Schools." *Nova Economia* 29 (2): 591–621.

APPENDIX

TABLE A1 Management practices measured across survey instruments

TYPES OF MANAGEMENT PRACTICES	MANAGEMENT-SPECIFIC SURVEYS DESIGNED BY RESEARCHERS			LARGE ADMINISTRATIVE EDUCATION SURVEYS	
	WMS	SDMS	TIME USE	PROVA BRASIL	PISA 2012
Establishing adequate incentives for teachers	x		x	x	x
Establishing appropriate plans and goals	x				x
Instilling a high-performance culture and rewarding good performers	x		x	x	x
Fostering leadership and engagement with stakeholders	x	x	x	x	x
Managing operational/administrative processes	x	x	x	x	x
Managing consequences for poor performance	x		x		
Managing social-emotional development			x		
Managing the school environment and its safety		x	x		
Monitoring organizational performance	x			x	x
Planning instructional processes	x	x	x	x	X

Note: WMS = World Management Survey (presented in Bloom and others 2015); SDMS = School Disaster Management Survey administered in Haiti (presented in Adelman, Baron, and Lemos, forthcoming). *Time use* refers to the time use survey administered in Brazil (Almeida and others, forthcoming). Prova Brasil is a large administrative dataset from Brazil (mapped in Leaver, Lemos, and Scur 2019). Questions in all surveys have been mapped using the 10 categories above or "not management."

REFERENCES

Adelman, Melissa, Juan Baron, and Renata Lemos. Forthcoming. "Managing Shocks in Education: Evidence from Hurricane Matthew in Haiti." Working paper, World Bank, Washington, DC.

Almeida, Rita, Leandro Costa, Ildo Lautharte, and Renata Lemos. Forthcoming. "Managerial Time Allocation and Student Learning: Evidence from Brazil." Working paper.

Bloom, Nicholas, Renata Lemos, Raffaella Sadun, and John Van Reenen. 2015. "Does Management Matter in Schools?" *The Economic Journal* 125 (584): 647–74.

Leaver, Clare, Renata Lemos, and Daniela Scur. 2019. "Measuring and Explaining Management in Schools: New Approaches Using Public Data." Policy Research Working Paper 9053, World Bank, Washington, DC.

www.ingramcontent.com/pod-product-compliance
Lightning Source LLC
Chambersburg PA
CBHW040533020526
44117CB00028B/22